AS THE CANOE TIPS

ALSO BY BILL CASSELMAN
from McARTHUR & COMPANY

Casselman's Canadian Words

Casselmania

Canadian Garden Words

Canadian Food Words

Canadian Sayings

What's in a Canadian Name?

Canadian Sayings 2

Canadian Sayings 3

AS THE CANOE TIPS

Comic Scenes from Canadian Life

BILL CASSELMAN

McArthur & Company
Toronto

Published in Canada in 2005 by
McArthur & Company
322 King St. West, Suite 402
Toronto, ON
M5V 1J2
www.mcarthur-co.com

Library and Archives Canada Cataloguing in Publication

Casselman, Bill, 1942-
        As the canoe tips : comic scenes from Canadian
life / Bill Casselman.

ISBN 1-55278-493-2

        1. Canadian wit and humor (English) I. Title.

FC173.C38 2005   C818'.602   C2005-900588-2

Cover Design by: Tania Craan
Composition and Design by: Tania Craan
Printed in Canada by: Transcontinental Printing

The publisher would like to acknowledge the financial support of the
Government of Canada through the Book Publishing Development
Program, The Canada Council for the Arts, and the Ontario
Government of Ontario through the Ontario Media Development
Corporation Ontario Book Initiative.

10 9 8 7 6 5 4 3 2 1

CONTENTS

Dedication v

Preface ix

PART 1
Funny Pieces 13

What's the difference between a Canuck and a canoe? Sometimes a canoe tips.

That old wheezer about Canadians being cheap is, of course, quite false. But we are funny. As the world turns, as the canoe tips, Canadians caught in the preservative amber of a guffaw are my goal here and my inspiration. These funny pieces have been safely tested on blind, albino gerbils. As youth preservatives and dewrinklers, they have proven better than Botox in Buffalo and cheaper than an eye job using a weed-eater.

In the first part of my book called "Funny Pieces" you'll meet characters out on a day pass from my subconscious. They were released for silly behaviour and on their own lack of cognizance. For example, there's Sincere Sid Kelp, Used Submarine Salesman of Portsmouth, England: "She's a yare little submersible. Perfect for you, matey. Canadian Navy, are you now? Well, you're a fine tar! This submarine I'm offering today has only been driven around the harbour twice, by a little old lady who seldom needed a submarine because she was born with gills. True as I'm standing here, mate. Fine then, you'll want to sign right here, sir." On second thought, I'm no longer certain that Sincere Sid made it into one of the stories.

You will encounter the kids at the cheap Haliburton aquarium who visit a burnt-out dolphin named Flippant. Poor Flippant just doesn't care anymore. He looks at the kiddies crowding around his tank, blows them an aquatic raspberry, and swims over to the far side of the tank. This summer the camp counsellors at Camp Shining Water took a pass on a Flippant visit. Last summer members of the Junior Good Guys Youth of Tomorrow Club had visited the dolphin and been apprehended in the act of teaching Flippant to ingest marijuana pellets hidden in a folded sardine.

There are exciting book reviews to catch up on in the first part as well, including *My Life in the Garden*, by Pillory Thrips-Gibbett. Here at last are the memoirs of Miss Thrips-Gibbett, the world's leading authority on ornamental thistles, who is also plucky Canadian-born headmistress of Kidneystoun, her no-nonsense gardening school for British girls, which is nestled in an old quarry in the Cotswolds. We've all read of Miss Pillory, who begins each semester by scraping the bare arms of her students repeatedly with crown-of-thorns branches and having all the girls chirp in unison, "Ouchies! Ouchies!" Also included is an instructive list of novel uses for those leftover lengths of garden twine that hang in the woodshed. These are detailed in her chapter entitled "Bondage Tips for School Leavers."

Those are a few appetizers for the wee feast. Enjoy more funny pieces inside.

Canadians have fun with the way they use language too, and some of that linguistic hilarity smiles through in "Words in My Life," Part 2 of this book, where my cosseted peeves get an airing and, I trust, a chuckle of recognition. Among other worthies in this section of the book, you meet the person who gave me the biggest laugh of my life.

I dedicate *As the Canoe Tips* to my only brother, Ron,

because I love him and because we share a very similar sense of Casselman humour, partly our own and partly a direct inheritance from the sunny nature of our father, Alfred Merkley Casselman. Dad was a teacher in a small town who was clever, verbal, and widely read. As he observed 40 years of the shenanigans of the citizens whose children he taught, my father brought home to our supper table a satirical eye that had spent the day teaching and watching the town's folly. Dad had one rule of humour that he never violated. He always said, "Don't laugh at them if they can't help it." I'm afraid I don't always follow that reasonable paternal advice, but I try. My brother Ron, on the other hand, adheres to Dad's rule.

Another guiding sentence of which I'm fond is one by the late Hunter S. Thompson: "When the going gets weird, the weird turn pro." Rest in pieces, gonzo guy and great writer.

P.T. Barnum said, "This way to the Egress!" That's the exit to the preface, but the entrance to the fun. There is satire here but I hope the main ingredient is the higher silliness, the sportive contrail of whimsy, the immodest gigglefest not to be seen by Uncle Fred, the banker with lips like a staple gun, or by Auntie Mildred, his wife, busy in the parlour now packaging overseas boxes of "Decency Band-Aids for Navel Oranges" so those sensitive people in Halooshistan don't have to be affronted by naked fruit.

I hope you have as much fun in this book as I did on my favourite boyhood ride in the Conklin sideshow at the Canadian National Exhibition. Imagine it's the end of a boy's summer on an August night in Toronto 50 years ago. The day was hot, but now a breeze from Lake Ontario pools in and skims across the CNE grounds.

Sure, sweat still pastes a plop of purple cotton candy to your right cheek and your tummy is at half-quease after 27 vertiginous revolvings of the giant Ferris wheel. But you're safe in the rattling pod car now, shuffling on clicketty tracks out of the Canadian twilight and into the cave of mirth on a ride called "Laugh in the Dark."

Bill Casselman
205 Helena Street,
Dunnville, Ontario, Canada
N1A 2S6

Email: canadiansayings@mountaincable.net
Website: www.billcasselman.com

PART 1
Funny Pieces

As the Canoe Tips

Selected Pages from a Summer Diary by a Counsellor
at Camp Shining Water

May 10

This will be my first diary written at camp. I'm not going
to write every day, just when something brilliant or really
stupid happens. I'll tell this diary when the bazaar of life
gets so bizarre that I have to write it down to keep control
of it, to tamp it back into place.

I'm a senior counsellor this summer at Camp Shining
Water. "Big shining water" is one of the suggested trans-
lations of the word *Ontario* in Iroquoian languages like
Mohawk, Huron, and Seneca. Staff get here early in May
to clean and prepare the site for the campers who arrive
June 28. We have to let the old camp shake off winter. In
its cedar buildings we mend the heavings and unfrostings
of spring.

I'm 18 this October and came here first ten years ago
as a junior camper.

What is it about some Ontarians graced by new spring
sun? Warmth gongs a deep bell in us and calls us North.
Life's pulse comes again and asks again like summer. A
keen flute thrills in our blood and one day we smell pine
resin and wafting lake wind right at the corner of Yonge
and Bloor. If ever we have spent vacation days "up
North," its magnet never ceases to draw the iron of our
joy. We flock north to sandpiper away summer after-
noons, pertly trotting narrow beaches, hiking Georgian

Bay's wind-swooned rocks, inspecting scooped-out inlets along Lake Superior, paddling beeperless canoes along granitic shorelines sculpted by a hand far defter than Brancusi's.

Come, says camp or cottage. Come, my chilly, winter-weary ones. Come, and I will lull you warm in the lap of my days. Come, there will be spans of sun on cheeks and little arms, and running, hallooing plunges off the end of the boy-screaming dock into the water-fighting, girl-kersplashing waves. Freckles will come out to play and so will your heart.

June 28

Campers' arrival day is also taking-leave-of-parents day. Stockbroker Howard Renson drives his son Jeremy to camp in a pale-lemon Porsche Boxter. Hey, if you've got it, flaunt it, baby! Seated in the lean citric machine, Mr. Renson opens the car door and beckons his son to approach for a goodbye hug.

Mr. Renson: (whispering) Jeremy, whatever happens: be a man. Follow my motto. Repeat it for me now, son.

Jeremy: (fakes naïveté by hesitantly chewing the tip of one finger) Gee, Dad. Uh. Would that be the one you use on Bay Street?

Mr. Renson: Sure, son, that's a good one.

Jeremy: "Cheat the client, never the partner?"

Mr. Renson: Shhhh! No, no, no. The other one.

Jeremy: "When in doubt, forge a colleague's name?"

Mr. Renson: Are you being a smarty-pants, Jer?

Jeremy: No. I don't think I could be and still be your son.

Mr. Renson: That's my boy. Be good now. See you Labour Day!

Eavesdroppers wonder if Howard Renson realizes that Jeremy is already about twice as clever as his father.

Last night, after the last parents had skedaddled back to Toronto, after the campers were unpacked and had been "de-hysterified" and were safely sleeping, about 25 of us counsellors snuck two cases of Molson's down past the boathouse and out around the point and we all sat on Screwing Rock, renewing friendships from last summer and meeting the new counsellors. Very little screwing takes place on Screwing Rock but it was named by the first campers in the early 1950s because in the midst of a broad expanse of grey gneiss there is a hollow in the rock into which a couple might fit. Everybody offers their impressions of the new kids and the new parents. Counsellors Nancy and Joan offer the grabbiest take on the day.

Nancy: Did you meet the Whittakers? *Primitivo!*

Joan: How primitive?

Nancy: Mrs. Whittaker carries her younger children in a fold of tissue attached to her abdomen!

Joan: My god! You mean . . .?

Nancy: Yes, Mrs. Whittaker is a marsupial. Of course, she's driving a Bentley, so we have to be nice.

July 8

A tradition at Camp Shining Water is going to town for a summer outing. Today four of us counsellors took the Juniors into Mutantville to visit a local point of interest. On the Pacific coast of Mexico, Ixtapa boasts a dolphinarium. Mutantville in the Haliburton Highlands of Ontario has its very own carpatorium where we were scheduled to pass two hours studying the "exciting underwater world of bottom-feeding fish."

"Does that mean they eat with their bums, sir?" said one little embryonic zoologist.

"They're a bunch of fat minnows, dork. Who cares?" sneered his older pal.

But, when Millie, our trip counsellor, phoned the carpatorium, the owner, Vern Nurtler, told her all the koi had been found belly up in the ornamental carp tank that morning. Someone had left the aquarium public address system on all night, tuned to CBC Radio's excellent overnight international service, and the goldfish had been forced to listen to several hours of Armenian nose-flute concerti. And, well, the koi had succumbed to terminal ennui while trying to find the nose flute entry in the *Grove Dictionary of Music.*

But Vern Nurtler is nothing if not accommodating. Vern said the kids could still visit his burnt-out dolphin, Flippant. Poor Flippant just doesn't care anymore. He looks at the kiddies crowding around his tank, blows them an aquatic raspberry, and swims over to the far side of the tank. This summer we took a pass on a Flippant visit. Last summer members of the Junior Good Guys Youth of Tomorrow Club had visited the dolphin and been apprehended in the act of teaching Flippant to ingest marijuana pellets hidden in a folded sardine.

However, camp counsellors are old hands at regrouping and rerouting, and you always have a backup plan. Instead we trundled all the Juniors off to another exciting local educational venue, the Cavalcade of Farm Machinery History Museum. It's just down Bay of Lakes Road, past Blistering Pines, the resort where they've had all that trouble with poison ivy. As they trooped in, we pointed out to the kids the fully restored early Ontario snake fence. It's remarkable how well-preserved those little reptile bodies are.

Inside the museum? A trove of our heritage: threshing machines, binder-twine scarecrows, steam-driven tractors, and Linda T. Osbertson. Yes! The same Linda T. Osbertson who, on the night of September 23, 2001, fed her husband, Ferlan Osbertson, into a hay-baling machine. Linda is right there in the museum and grants interviews to interested visitors from her rocking chair beside the actual hay-baler. "Fit of pique, it was," says Linda, with some regret. "Came over me sudden-like, when I caught Ferlan with the hired hand. Looked real too, that hand. Made of plastic though. Thing is, I jus' didn't care fer what Ferland was doin' with it."

With visions of Massey and Harris and Ferguson dancing in our tired noggins, at 5 o'clock we all piled into the old school bus and headed back to Camp Shining Water for supper, taking the scenic road along Bay of

Lakes, where it meets Lake Water, over the Wet River bridge, along Bay of Shorelines, through the hamlet of Moistbrook, past Thane of Cawdor RV Camp, and finally we turned that last bend at Slightly Damp Creek, and so to bed, as Pepys would say.

August 8

In the course of a long summer, every camp loses a counsellor or two, and Camp Shining Water is no exception. Today we had to bid farewell to Becky Hudson who was sent home for barratry. This is a term in marine law for criminal behaviour by a member of the crew that is injurious or prejudicial to the ship's owner. It happened across the lake at the religious summer place. Camp Lackanookie is run by the First Church of Wendel, the Insurance Salesman. It's a small denomination from Listowel. Every summer we have a motorboat race with them, not on our lake which is mercifully motorboat-free, but on a long thin little lake about five kilometres from the camp. Quite early on the morning of the big race Becky had swabbed the exterior of their boat with a particularly volatile accelerant. When Mimsy Rowe and Dropsy Sheldon started their big twin Mercury outboards, they were blown over the finish line and won the race before it started.

We interviewed new recruits after breakfast at a long table in the dining room. As a senior counsellor I assisted in interviewing applicants. First up today was Jürgen von Pflickmesser, a 44-year-old recent immigrant whom Canada has welcomed from the former East Germany. The interview consists of test situations to which the applicants must supply apt answers indicating their training in teaching children, their knowledge of child psychology, and their love of guiding young persons toward a happy and productive future. I'll quote to you, diary, how the session began.

Camp Director: Bill, I'll let you begin the interview with candidate number one. Jean, will you kindly show a Mr. Jürgen von Pflickmesser into the room, please?

The introductions took place and Mr. Pflickmesser sat down.

Bill: We like to begin these informal and we hope friendly little chats by asking you, Mr. von Pflickmesser, if you have a question you would like to ask us?

Jürgen: *Ja!* I haf. Can I be assured this interview will not be stained by racist preconceptions about German people? Assured there will be no Nazi jokes and dat kind of garbage?

Bill: I speak for everyone at this table when I assure you no such stereotyping will take place.

Jürgen: *Gut!*

The candidate then extracts an exquisite, grey porcelain Glock from his hunting jacket, checks to insure that the gun is loaded, and puts the handgun inside his lunch bucket. He places the lunch bucket on the table in front of him.

Bill: Good Morning! May I call you Jürgen?

Jürgen: You may call me *Oberstabsfeldwebel von Pflickmesser!*

Bill: Sort of a Regimental Sergeant Major, eh? I'm sorry, sir, but we do not recognize Vopo titles of rank. Now that the East German Communist *Volkspolizei* or 'people's police' have been permanently disbanded, such titles are meaningless.

Jürgen: *Sehr gut!* Ven I want a retelling of the history that I myself have just lived through, I'll be sure to ask you, Bill.

Bill: Let's say young Freddy has wet his bed every night since arriving at camp? Mr. von Pflickmesser, what would you do with young Freddy?

Jürgen: Vee vud modify the *kleiner* Freddy's behaviour.

Bill: How would you accomplish that laudable goal?

Jürgen: First, vee wud tell the boy not to piss in his bed.

Bill: But if he continued to do so?

Jürgen: Vee vud rub his nose in the urine-soaked bedding, as one does mit a German Shepherd.

Bill: This is a nine-year-old child from a broken home.

Jürgen: He should have fixed the home before he set out for camp.

Bill: But still Freddy's urinary incontinence continues.

Jürgen: Vee vud be forced to withhold essential camp nutrients.

Bill: Such as?

Jürgen: Jellybeans, Shredded Wheat, and Ecstasy.

Bill: WHAT!

Jürgen: It vas a joke.

Bill: It's now Week Three and Freddy is still going wee-wee in the comforter.

Jürgen: Vee vud electrify the comforter, zo dat a mild but bracing electric shock vas delivered to the urinating miscreant.

Bill: If that "treatment" did not work, what then?

Jürgen: Vee vud haf to stop farting about with decadent Western coddling of young persons and proceed to more effective methods.

Bill: What would that mean?

Jürgen: Freddy vud be crucified to the door of Cabin Number 3, mein Herr!

Camp Director: Well—I'll take over here, Bill—thank you very much, Mr. Pflickmesser. We'll let you know.

August 10

Another birdwatching day! The campers love it. The ones who don't care for our winged friends have fun making up new names for their life lists. Here are a few of mine. The most prominent birdcall was that of the Interminable Chat. It would not stop its strange 'feeple-feeple' noise. Also flitting through the pubertal green down of early-leafing trees and shrubs could be seen that unfortunate bird that keeps getting stuck to creosote deposits, the Chimney Slow.

My life list of Canadian birds includes:
The Overpriced Summer Petrol
The Liberal Gull (common Canadian bird)
The Common Dildo or Woodcock
The Still Bittern (after all these years)
The Management-Hating BobWhite
The Primal-Scene Gross-Peek
The Chaffed Dickthistle
The Nun-Spotting Cloistercatcher
and, finally,
The Popeyed and Olivaceous Cormorant.

August 12

It's arts and crafts week at Camp Shining Water! Wee! Be still, my plaster of Paris heart! Special treats include Kozy Kraft Korner, conducted by sewing mistress Mary Quent, nicknamed "Our Lady of Perpetual Needles." Rumour spread by the senior counsellor girls claims that Miss

Quent is quite frigid in bed, but is able to experience the rare "Quilt" orgasm, obtained by running the hands over patches of gingham and muslin.

This week we are privileged to have artists in residence for five days. The children's special fave is the Estonian mime artist Katya Tonik who has a papier-mâché installation in front of the kitchen called "The Mountain of Me." One morning, as breakfast finishes and the campers pour out of the dining room heading for canoe lessons and rush past the installation without a look, Mrs. Tonik screams, "Look! I'm a boulder." One young lad wearing Oakley Why 3 sunglasses stops, takes off his expensive shades, and says, "No, Mrs. Tonik, you are a nutbar sitting on a grey pillow." His silvery laughter trails him down to the canoe-ribbed dock. The kids have nicknames for everyone. Poor Mrs. Tonik, for all her earnest efforts to open the world of mime and jazz dance to the children, is known to them as "ElastoSpaz."

The Friday of arts and crafts week is a special travel day that we like to call "The World Outside Camp." These are day trips with the kids designed to broaden the urban child's experience of the world. Today we are visiting local artists. First stop is a trendy shop in town called Death, Be Not Dull. Inside are handwoven shrouds for all occasions. And there at her spinning clay wheel is the county's most prominent ceramicist, Maud-Lynn Luguber. Maudie's specialty is ceramic cremation urns featured like the departed, a sort of funerary Toby mug. Mrs. Luguber crafts each urn-mug from a cherished photograph of your departed loved one. Next door is Let Nature Dress You! operated by the artist Millicent Curlew. These are fashion statements to make Rodeo Drive green with envy.

A popular seller is Millicent's sumac-leaf dirndl or a delicious artist's frock made entirely from woven pigweed strands. Hubbie is not neglected either. Why not take back to the city a birchbark kilt? Perfect for the man who wants to wear something different to a Blue Jays game.

On the way home we had one hour left that permitted us to let the campers visit the Old Cedar Bog near Nurtler, Ontario. The Slough of Despond has nothing on Nurtler's Old Cedar Bog. A flatboat poled by Ezra Nurtler himself takes the children on a scenic excursion across the glutinous surface of the bog. Ezra is a fountain of local stories: "There be bundles throwed into this here swamp that no Christian person would ever want to open. Nosiree!" When a palsied hand rose and sank three times into the bog, visions of King Arthur's Excalibur and the Lady in the Lake danced in our heads.

September 2, Last Day of Camp

Wonder held our breath all through July and August and summer brimmed with awe. The kids grew brown and wise and happy. There were no fatalities and only a few injuries. There was one great victory. We went to County Council and beat the Cottagers' Association who wanted to put motorboats on the lake. We fought off the owner of the 12 hardware stores whose moronic, hairy sons think summer is dead unless twin outboard motors can be strapped to a Popsicle stick and revved all day long back and forth across the frightened lake, shredding its piney silence.

My philosophical musing from this summer's thought-pool is a minor wave indeed, but here it is. As the canoe tips you may all be certain of one consequence:

you're going to get your ass wet. Enjoy therefore the ride across the lake. Contrary to the daydreams of the cross-clutchers, it is not a return voyage. When the canoe tips, that dude in the stern is not your kindly pa; it's Charon, boatman of the Styx. He's not handing you a new oar. He's holding a scythe.

Now summer camp season has passed. In autumn, birches throw yellow leaves across the path down to the boathouse. Slender maple saplings flame orange beside the creek. I believe these trees are meant to do this blanketing in solitude, with few sounds from the camp. Oh, maybe the lubb-dupp of a window shutter forgotten during the last day's frantic rush to lock the camp up for winter.

Now the car is by the gate. Take one look back. The lake breeze freshens and dry summer grasses, bled brittle by autumn, hum strummed by the wind. It behooves us to tiptoe from this scene like obedient extras. For in this forlorn and lovely mellowing of the year, we are out-of-season; we are intruders in the must of fall.

I am often accosted on the common way by low-born persons seeking to learn the genteel method of discharging nasal mucus. It is, of course, a topic of some delicacy and not to be broached near to or immediately after a meal, particularly if the repast consists of thickish onion soup. At the same time I feel safe in declaring that the wanton blowing of the nose is universally deprecated.

And yet pillars of social rectitude like Emily Post in a long career devoted to telling humanity how to behave, even sweet Emily failed to offer cogent nose advice. In our own era Letitia Baldrige (one 'd' please) and Miss Manners have been meanly silent on the proper mode of keeping one's nostrils gracefully absterged. *Absterge* is the correct verb; it means 'to clean by wiping.'

Some of us, born in the Upper Jurassic era and still wearing raptor-tooth necklaces, may remember nasal-care posters in the nurse's office at public school. Usually a large, smiling, entirely bumptious nose, depicted in garish flesh colours, waved from the poster in your upturned child's face, the nose's odious little stick hands carrying a handkerchief. The caption bubble said, "Hi Kiddies! I'm Happy Nose! I'm NEVER WET & DRIPPY 'cause Mom packs Kleenex in my lunchbox!" But no gestural tips were given concerning how best to attain clean nostrils. Just how best to purchase nasal tissues.

A socially acceptable method of nasal cleansing exists, but few know it. Fewer still practise it. Were you aware, for instance, of the small but permissible range of sounds that may be emitted during polite nose blowing? I thought not. It's best then if you keep reading. For detailed in this essay are these sounds and other neglected mucous minutiae.

All persons of status and merit ought to know how to blow their noses, for the aftermath of slovenly nose-blowing can devastate a wardrobe. Imagine! Suddenly you are summoned to Rideau Hall to be invested into that august company of Canadian immortals known as the Ordure of Canada. On the eve of your elevation to a status just this side of Stockwell Day, you discover with unutterable horror that apparel made of triple cashmere and necessary for your investiture is encrusted with dried, once-projectile *materia nasalis* from that afternoon when the pepper-grinder exploded. Quite a sad afternoon. For he was a pleasant little man and a cheerful servant, that pepper-grinder. Italian, I think.

But I want to keep this article on the nose. It is best to begin, if not at the beginning, then at a place that will darn well fool most of the listening bozos into thinking that it is the beginning. So, class, do I have your attention? If I don't, an electric cattle prod will soon pass over your somnolent noggins. To begin then, our first knowledge of the nose, as an historical entity, comes from a temple inscription found in early Rome, New York, in 1896. On Murphy Street beside the tire factory, we find on the outer pillar, the one marked "Men," these words: *SACER EST LOCUS. EXTRA EMUNGITE.*

The translation from Latin: 'This place is holy. Blow your nose outside.'

No one at the nearby University of Rochester seems to know why this inscription is there, but it does imply the existence of the nose and suggests that, however backward upstate New Yorkers may have been, at Rome by 1896 they had discovered their noses.

Further elucidation (but not much) appears in the little-known Platonic dialogue *De Emunctione*, "A Disquisition upon Blowing the Nose," in which that remarkable Greek Mnphthps and his pal Mykteros seek from Socrates the most virtuous method of blowing the nose. Now Socrates does not have a **lot** to say to the two youths, beyond pointing out that to him (Socrates) a boy's nostrils have always seemed more virtuous than a girl's. Mnphthps and Mykteros take one look at Socrates, wrap their tunics (chitons, actually) tightly around their butts and run off quickly down the street to another philosopher who has promised to teach Mnphthps how to say his name aloud without swallowing his tongue.

I admit that all the palaver heretofore does not get us too far along the road of nose knowledge. But what's that old British saying? All work and no play with nose to the grindstone make Jack have to breathe through his ear? Perhaps I have only the gist of the saying? For a detailed study of the dialogue I suggest *Socratic Rhinology for the Home*, a popular guide published in 1890 by a Victorian divine, an Anglican vicar, the Very Reverend Doctor Flinders Mellowood who almost became Archbishop of Canterbury but was voted down at the last minute when the High Church selection committee learned that Mellowood's hobby on weekends was conducting nude tours of the estuaries of English rivers.

Before presenting the details of decorous emunction, I have thought it best to touch briefly on the nose in great literature. The most celebrated nasal stanzas occur in the dialect poems of the Scottish poet, Robert MacRogaster (often dismissed as second-degree Burns). MacRogaster's verses attain a harmony that indicates clearly they were composed on a used comb. We quote his immortal line from "Lad of Dunderboom":

> *Oug wi' hyeh spree 'fer in a wuh.'*

Has anything more redolent of a blown nostril ever been written?

What schoolboy has not stood on a gusty night, reciting to the winds these lines found in Harley Ferk's *Teach Your Children Armenian after Work*?

> *O! That big ol' nose.*
> *O! That big ol' nose.*
> *O! That big ol' ol' nose.*

Who dare forget the nose in sculpture? Think of Luccio's "The Meditation of the Earl of Sheffield After the Battle of Schpurtzenflegel," the noble head resting on the back of the Queen Anne armchair, the great brow furled, the text of the *Iliad* in Greek lying open upon the general's lap, the third digit of the general's left hand reposing gracefully within the confines of his right nostril.

The crux of my advice on how to blow your nose is strict adherence to a system of "nose noise" which classifies the vulgarity of the act by the sound issuing from the nasal passages during emunction. And here it is:

1. **Honk** – utterly crass and vulgar
2. **Snuzz** – bourgeois, hints of social climbing
3. **Ploip** – a light ploip never out of place among the high middle class
4. **Hhnurr** – aristocratic and by far most pleasing to listeners' ears

Let this infallible guide accompany you and your nose through life. It was taught to your humble deponent by a person who must remain forever nameless. Well, almost. I say nameless, but when I last encountered the lady she was helping the police force of Buffalo, New York, with certain inquiries and was known to their officers as Tonawanda Wanda.

HYPOCHONDROL

The drug that is all side effects with no effective main purpose
Doesn't cure anything!
Total Lack of Efficacy!
No Known Major Results!
Alleviates nothing!

Hypochondrol, available as a gel cap, is a superb medication, a new drug from RTM Inc. especially for hypochondriacs, completely tested on four Albanian shepherds for more than 12 minutes. Hypochondrol will promote in most users these **guaranteed side effects:**

- Unease
- Minor constipation
- Dizziness
- Hives
- Gas
- Heartburn
- Oil
- Tar sands
- Hollow feeling that you neglected to put on underwear
- Indigestion
- Falling coat
- Upset stomach
- Runny nose
- Leaf mould
- Underarm rash
- Hot flashes
- Excessive blinking
- Minor hair loss
- Green around the vent (a symptom usually confined to egg-laying chickens)
- Dry mouth
- Wet sink
- Untidy closet

- Diarrhea
- Vomiting
- Highland dancing
- Scurvy
- Ring worm
- Cold sores
- Real worry about the size and roseate hue of Ralph Klein's nose
- Gulping
- Mild fever
- Sensitivity to bright light
- Sick feeling of wanting to vote for Stephen Harper
- Just a few heart palpitations
- Intermittent coughing
- Illegal cheerleader palpitations
- Listlessness
- Indifference
- Occasional inability to read a map of Germany
- Lack of interest in sex
- Quickened heartbeat brought on by thinking about giving up hypochondria

*Please note that in our totally blind tests there is only one major side effect: not being born, if taken by your pregnant mother.

Another result of careful laboratory research from dedicated scientists at

RUSH TO MARKET INC.
RTM
Our motto: "New drugs way before they're ready"

LLOYD'S ISSUES
A Dialogue Scene from Village Life

Exterior. Aerial slo-mo camera glides through large fluffy white clouds, angling down towards earth. A very large white cloud fills the entire frame.

Optical white-in to:

Exterior. Summer. Tree-lined street in small Canadian town. TWO MIDDLE-AGED WOMEN chat amiably at the end of a sidewalk leading to a slightly rundown house.

WIFE
Lloyd has anger management issues.

SYMPATHETIC NEIGHBOUR LADY
What happened?

WIFE
Lloyd got nine years for manslaughter.

NEIGHBOUR LADY
My, them judges is harsh. Lloyd's paid his dues before for that other misunderstanding.

WIFE
I coulda sworn that baby fell into the cement mixer.

It wasn't Lloyd's fault. He was doing his best.
Considerin' how much heroin Lloyd injected that morning before turning the cement mixer on.

NEIGHBOUR LADY
The fuss that trash made about that baby. You'd think it was their only child.

WIFE
It was.

NEIGHBOUR LADY
That child might have died of boredom later in life. Never can tell. What happened this time with Lloyd?

WIFE
Lloyd was digging peacefully in the back garden.
Minding his own business.

NEIGHBOUR LADY
The way he does. When he's out on a day pass.

WIFE
So this elderly woman came over and asked Lloyd for directions to the hospital.

NEIGHBOUR LADY
That can be so off-putting.

WIFE
The old bat asked him twice.

NEIGHBOUR LADY
The nerve!

WIFE
Why, Lloyd said he could hardly understand her with all
that portable oxygen tube stuff in her nose.

NEIGHBOUR LADY
Sick people are so pushy nowadays.

WIFE
Well, what could Lloyd do? To stop her chattering on
and on like that, Lloyd gave her a tap on the head with
his garden shovel.

NEIGHBOUR LADY
A person of Lloyd's intelligence deserves to get a word in
edgewise once in a while.

WIFE
You'd a thought that old bat was the Queen of Sheba or
something, the way she just fell over dead so quick.

NEIGHBOUR LADY
I bet you a dime to a doughnut she was poorly to begin
with. All that oxygen tubing.

WIFE
You could tell she was the kind that don't look after
themselves properly. Yep, she up and fell into Lloyd's pile
of dug-up onions and died right on the spot.

NEIGHBOUR LADY
No respect for other people's property at all.

WIFE
Died even before that nosy neighbour, Mrs. Orsin, could
phone the police.

NEIGHBOUR LADY
Helen Orsin has no life of her own. That's why she's so
nosy.

WIFE
Claimed her poodle ran through the old lady's blood
and tracked it all over her so-called Persian rug.

NEIGHBOUR LADY
Are they Iraqi, those Persian rugs?

WIFE
Lloyd could hardly eat that prison food for his first
months in jail. Throwed him off his normal appetite.
Upset him no end, that jury verdict after only two
minutes of so-called dee-liberation.

NEIGHBOUR LADY
That old biddy died just to cause trouble.

WIFE
Lloyd'll never do carefree, happy garden work again.

NEIGHBOUR LADY
Where's Lloyd today? I saw him downtown yesterday.

WIFE
Yeah you did. But they took him away.

NEIGHBOUR LADY
No!

WIFE
You know that shrink, that head doctor they had him
goin' to every damn week?

NEIGHBOUR LADY
Not Lloyd? How humiliating! Like as if Lloyd were some
kind of common criminal psycho nut case.

WIFE
Well, as I say, if you'll let me continue, Lloyd was in
anger class.

NEIGHBOUR LADY
Yeah?

WIFE
When Lloyd and the shrink got into a tussle over how
many people Lloyd had wounded or killed.

NEIGHBOUR LADY
How awful!

WIFE
And Lloyd cut three fingers off the doctor's hand.

NEIGHBOUR LADY
Got in the way, did it?

WIFE
Way Lloyd tells it, the doc was holding up his hand as he quoted from Lloyd's police record.

NEIGHBOUR LADY
Them doctors. They're all flighty.

Cut (Throat)

1. **Embraced By the Blight,** by Betsy-Wetsy Nurtler, Crystal Research Press, $29.95. Mrs. Nurtler has travelled far from the tentative probings in her first book on plant afterlife, *I'd Like to Be an Atheist, But I'm Subject to Black Spot.* Mope no more over the corpse of that antique peony that succumbed to drought. Here Betsy-Wetsy offers definite proof that plants don't die. No, dears, they go up to Green Heaven, don little white nighties and winglets, and flit about the upper ethers for oh! such a long time.

2. **Scottish Gardening,** by Sir Hamish McSphincter, Loch Daft Publications, $34.50. Riveting anecdotes about hybrid gorse and his renowned "wee scraggle o' heather" look. McSphincter is candid about the famous scandal too. Sir Hamish admits he did perforate his only son with a backhoe. But, as he says, it was done in a fit of pique.

3. **Hiring Garden Help**, no author listed, Ontario Department of Correctional Institutes Press, $9.50. Plain talk about the delicacy of employer-employee relationships in horticultural work. I myself make it an absolute rule never to argue with any handyman nicknamed "Pigsticker." If Glenda, "the matron's earth assistant,"

states that she can only do the rose garden Fridays because she's out on a day pass, do pay heed.

4. My Life in the Garden, by Pillory Thrips-Gibbett, Stone Books, $23. Here at last are the memoirs of Miss Thrips-Gibbett, the world's leading authority on ornamental thistles, who is also plucky headmistress of Kidneystoun, her no-nonsense gardening school for British girls nestled in an old quarry in the Cotswolds. We've all read of Miss Pillory, who begins each semester by scraping the bare arms of her students repeatedly with crown-of-thorns branches and having all the girls chirp in unison, "Ouchies! Ouchies!" One amusing chapter details the invention of the High-Allergy Straw Gardening Hat by three of Miss Thrips-Gibbett's star pupils: Mimsy, Muffy, and Dropsy. Also included is an instructive list of novel uses for those leftover lengths of garden twine that hang in the woodshed. These are detailed in her chapter entitled "Bondage Tips for School Leavers."

5. The Zen of Landscrape: A Philosophy of Northern Soil Management, by Lars Thorwaldssen, Bleak House, $19.95. Clinical depression did not stop Lars from offering a bracing new vista to homeowners wanting something original in property design. Lars explains the joy of bulldozing off all the topsoil of your land and learning to enjoy the dried, lifeless clay substrate that remains. "What, after all," says Lars, "is life?" This book was completed by Lars's widow and was published from the profits on the patent to Lars's chemical discovery, Hort-Mort. A quick spray from the leaky aerosol container establishes a pleasing life-free zone within 200 yards of any dwelling.

6. Heirloom Weeds, by Anthony Deatlea, Verdure Press, $25.99. Get *au courant* with the latest gardening trend and pick up cultivation tips for all manner of floral bizarrerie. For example, you'll learn how to grow the now-largely-unknown scourge of the Regency parterre, twatwort, also called pudendimums. Diligently, Anthony has searched the world for neglected, exotic weeds including the East Borneo carnivorous fern, the one that sticks to a dog's elevated hind leg, dissolves the interior flesh, and sucks it into the plant's vascular system through thousands of little ingestive cups called sarco-haustoria. A must for urban flower beds.

7. Cured!, by Anonymous, Mustard Seed Books, $19. The author is the first successful graduate of the Impatiens Rehab Centre in Ontario's lush Caledon Hills. The author explains how each addict is treated, leading the reader carefully through the full therapy, including the tiny electrodes attached to the trowel, so that each time the addict digs a hole to plant an impatiens, a mild but bracing electric shock is delivered, until soon those under care graduate and receive their badges as true impatients.

8. Stud Whomp: How Men Weed, by Hortensio Viagrelli, Musk Press, $25. Has that charming fen at the bottom of your property suffered invasion by purple loosestrife? Don't putter and fumble with chemical eradicants. Simply eyeball the Internet site of *Soldier of Fortune* magazine, and order a flamethrower. Or perhaps consider another of Mr. Viagrelli's notions, something he calls his "organic weed eater." At Devastazione, his remote ancestral hilltop in southern Italy, Viagrelli has revived the concept of a living ornamental dwarf. A tiny gentleman named Luigi inhabits a grotto on the estate and can be seen by visitors on weekdays. He is easily identified by his green teeth and dandelion breath. For after the weeding, Viagrelli markets his own brand of fertilizer, but is coy about the contents, saying only "the mixture in my product will grow hair on a wooden leg in three days." Luckily, I keep a wooden leg on a rack in my garage for purposes of scientific verification, and shall test it soon.

9. Really Rare Seeds, by Fritz Dampfinghoff, Eureka Books, $14.95. Something for the devout garden snob. These seeds of botanical exotica are not available in garden stores or by mail or courier. Instead—the last word in exclusive rarities—the seeds are delivered to Canada after Fritz glues them to the wings of specially trained, migrating locusts that fly them directly to your back door so your snotty gardening neighbours can't see what is delivered or ever know how you received the seeds.

How do Canadian villages and towns receive their names? In this little story, I answer the question "How did Mibbley Falls get its name?"

When the first crew of TV reporters arrived at the high school from the city, one of them asked, "If this is Mibbley Falls, then where's the waterfall?" A reasonable question and one most people wonder about sooner or later during a sojourn here.

How did Mibbley Falls get its name when there is no waterfall larger than a parson's pee stream for one hundred miles around? In 1831, Cephrenus Mibbley, a miller newly arrived from the border country of southern Scotland, built the first gristmill on the lower Turtle River. He was able to deepen a stream, divert river water, and construct a millrace whose powerful torque could turn the great wooden wheel of the mill.

Now Cephrenus was fond of a wee dram at eventide, and for a very particular reason. So he put up behind his mill a snug shed to house a copper still. After a year and three months of tongue-on experimentation, the old Scot had become a dab hand at sour mash preparation. Soon he had confected, in the wilderness, an amber distillate potent enough to corrugate a grown man's larynx. His tipple became known locally as "Sluice Juice" and was the medicinal restorative of choice throughout the entire county. Said one customer, a farmer who passed the mill on the way into Oughtville for weekly supplies, "Jar o' Sluice Juice'd take rust off a car's bumper in one minute."

One night, about 15 years after the building of his mill, Cephrenus drank a few dippers too many of his own firewater and got stiff as a fresh-boiled owl, yet he prepared to set out on his nightly rounds, a traipse over his property to insure that the mill was safely tucked in for the evening. Skedaddle out of the house he did every night, stepping faster than a hen on a hot griddle, impelled by one motive: to escape Annie.

After his wife's supper table had been cleared and her dishes had been washed and put away, it was Annie's habit to sit at the kitchen table and read aloud from her King James Bible by the light of an oil lamp. "'And Joktan begat Almodad, and Sheleph, and Hazarmaveth, and Jerah.'"

Hearing her begin the begats, Cephrenus spat tobacco juice into the fireplace, with all the propulsive, labial contempt his pucker could muster. "Och, them holy men and women certainly fornicated like minks."

"Language!" snapped Annie.

"And the Almighty encouraged those crabby shepherds. They had a serious population problem. Their god didn't have enough altar-lickers."

"Let the devil do his own talking, Cephrenus."

"Keep humping, sayeth the Lord."

Annie wagged a finger at her husband.

"Mind," said Cephrenus, "the pioneer righteous had nay but time for all that belly-slappin' what with Goddamn manna crashing down upon their heads every time the poor buggers looked up to see if rain was coming.

Never mind the bread on the roof, O Lord. Where's the wee hairy hole?"

Annie stamped one foot on the log floor. "Ceph Mibbley, you'll not blaspheme in your cups under this roof. Is that clear?"

A silence fell in the kitchen. Loudly, Cephrenus slurped from his dipper of homemade whisky. Annie picked up her Bible and began to read again: "'And Hadoram, and Uzal, and Diklah. And Obal, and Abimael, and Sheba. And Ophir, and Havilah, and Jobab: all these were the sons of Joktan.'"

"Wee Jock was quite the stickman, then. Och, it's all brainless twaddle. Can ye no see, Annie, that religion is a crib for wee bairns to sleep in? It's the great tit in the sky, with billions squollerin' for a suck, a drop, of the magic milk that will banish death. Do ye not ken that such milk comes out sour? Because immortality is a monstrous great fib."

Annie interrupted and spoke louder, "'All these were the sons of Joktan.'"

"So ye said, woman. Well, Joktan got his ha'penny every night, did he not? Meself now, I'd like to give you a dig in the whiskers now and then, lassie. But I'd have to pry the Good Book off it, wouldn't I now? Just to get past the wet gates."

Cephrenus was a bandy-legged little Scot about four feet nine inches tall, while Annie was six feet two inches.

"'And Peleg lived thirty years and begat Reu. And Peleg lived after he begat Reu two hundred and nine years, and begat sons and daughters. And Reu lived two and thirty years, and begat Serug.'"

From his dipper the tiny Cephrenus sucked another

stiff swig of homebrew, and said, "I've a notion this night, Annie, to kick your arse."

"You'd have to do some mighty high steppin' to accomplish that feat, Ceph Mibbley."

"Ay, I would too. But I'm off now."

"You're intoxicated. Be careful, Ceph. I love you and so does God."

"Bejaisus then, maybe He'll bend over for a quick thrust up the old shit-shute?"

Annie stiffened in her chair. "'Then the Lord rained upon Sodom and upon Gomorrah brimstone and fire out of heaven.'"

After he slammed the kitchen door, Cephrenus inhaled deeply, "Ahh. Bonnie breeze, and not a word of holy drivel on the night wind." Sipping again from the dipper of hootch he'd taken with him, the red-haired miller walked quickly back the entire length of the mill-stream. He stumbled once, because he was all fucky-toed with drink, like a horse in a patch of ripe pumpkins. Just at the start of the millrace, where the water quickened, he tripped on a tree root and fell into the stream.

At 66, he was not as hale as he had been nor had he ever been a competent swimmer. Cephrenus was startled at the speed with which the water carried him away. As he was swept down the race, he scraped his bum on the rocks lining the stream bottom, and when he reached out to grab for some underwater hold, skin was flayed off his fingers. Cephrenus yelped in pain, and the water seized the dipper from his hand and shot it downstream. Rather slowly it occurred to him that he must scream: "Bejaisus, Annie! Will ye no save me?"

No answer came from the house. The wind did carry a dissolved drone:

"'These are the sons of Seir the Horite, who inhabited the land; Lotan, and Shobal, and Zibeon, and Anah.'"

"Heeeelllp!"

"'And Dishon, and Ezer, and Dishan: these are the dukes of the Horites, the children of Seir in the land of Edom.'"

Outside, borne away on purling billows of death, Cephrenus yelled, "Get your twat out of Holy Writ and save me, ye useless drab!"

"'And Husham died, and Hadad the son of Bedad, who smote Midian in the field of Moab, reigned in his stead.'"

The metal dipper was sucked into the sluice and drawn under the mill wheel. With a sharp *scrak!* it was squished flatter than a slug under a wagon wheel.

Cephrenus tried a frantic dog-paddle and glubbed water. Choking, frightened, angry, he roared from the water, looking at the candlelight in the kitchen window, "Annie, you'd give a dog's arse heartburn." This was somewhat ungrateful because Annie kept a lit taper in the window solely to guide her husband home from his rounds after dark.

Propelled by the churning slats of the mill wheel the flattened dipper shot into the air and splashed down in the water near Cephrenus. "A whore's luck I have. My best dipper too."

As she recited the begats each night after her husband left the house, Annie tweaked each of her nipples in turn and repeatedly, decorously too of course, through the thick homespun of her work dress. It was an absent-minded gesture, perhaps to her scarcely a sexual one at all, one she hardly knew she did. "'Duke Kenaz, duke Teman, duke Mibzar, ahhhhh, duke Magdiel, duke Iram: these be the dukes of Edom.' Oh. Yes."

"Ay. Just squat there, Annie, like a fly on a fresh turd. While I drown, you silly big bitch!"

Then up ahead Cephrenus saw a chance. A white birch tree was half fallen over the course of the stream. The man reared up out of the sweeping water and used his utmost effort to stretch and grasp at the tree trunk. He grabbed it solidly. But the wood was punky. The rotten tree broke in his hands and he plunged back fully into the darkening waves. The water closed over him. And there was no sound but the idiot gurgle of the current. Suddenly, Cephrenus' head bobbed up briefly. He looked quite surprised to be drowning. He said, "Damn ye to a choiring hell of off-key angels, Annie McLeod!" He swallowed a terrifying gulp of water, sputtered, and sank. The throaty chuckle of the water filled the streamside air. Again his head bobbed up. The tree trunk, spun into alignment with the current's flow, came around and smacked Cephrenus squarely on the top of his skull. His eyes rolled upward. Nearer to the house now, the last earthly words he heard were: "'And the sons of Benjamin were Beulah, and Becher, and Ashbel, Gera, and Naaman, Ehi, and Rosh, and Muppim and Huppim, and Ard.'"

The last earthly thought of Cephrenus Mibbley was, *There's a full gallon of fine brew in that shed and it never felt a tongue.* Then an obtruding bolt of water gagged him and he lost consciousness and died.

The white birch trunk skimmed ahead of the heavier human body, hit a swollen, sodden bank of the millrace and jammed into the mud. Then the corpse of the drowned man slammed into the lodged tree trunk, and the force of the water pushed the body so that the corpse slumped over the tree, almost as if Cephrenus were straddling the tree for a happy ride downstream. The rush of waters around and over this bizarre obstacle created a minuscule waterfall, sadly the only one ever to cascade in the county.

An hour later, Annie came out and found her husband's corpse. She saddled up Old Queenie and rode to a neighbour's farm through the dark, weeping and empty, with no comfort save the heart's ease of the Good Book: "'And Arphaxad lived after he begat Salah four hundred and three years.'"

Annie brought back three stout farmhands to haul the body out of the water. It wasn't until the men were gone, and Cephrenus was lying blue and dead on the bed, that she could bring herself to pray, "Forgive my Ceph, Jesus, an errant sinner who spoke against the Light. Please hold him now, so safe, in your loving arms."

One of the farmhands, the first to see Cephrenus slung over the tree trunk in midstream, took one glance at the scene and dubbed it "Mibbley Falls" and the name stuck, like snot up a rooster's beak.

Here is a list of scientific phrases commonly found in academic journals and lab reports. Following each phrase is my translation of what the gobbledygook might actually mean.

"IT HAS LONG BEEN KNOWN THAT . . ." Translation: I couldn't find the damn journal article to cite. Claudia shredded it by mistake, placed it in a pile on the lunch table in the lab cafeteria, and Walt Elson's wife wore it home as a hairpiece. She was just released from Happy Walls, so we all understand, of course.

"A LOCATIVE TREND OF DEFINITIVE DIRECTION BECOMES EVIDENT UPON PERUSAL." Translation: This data is utterly fucking meaningless, but I have nothing else to insert here.

"WHILE IT HAS NOT BEEN POSSIBLE TO PROVIDE CONCRETIZED COHERENT RESPONSES BASAL TO THE INITIAL INQUIRY . . ." Translation: My series of important experiments concerning defecatory frequency in startled rodents failed in its early stages. The tinted, numbered voles tiptoed up to the entry point of the maze, peeked in, and promptly fell dead of ennui. Dirty little quitters. But I understand from colleagues that your journal is desperate and there's a good chance sheepheads like you will publish my garbage. Why in heaven did you ever name a recondite biochemistry journal *Annals of Excreta*?

"A TRIAD OF EXEMPLA WAS SELECTED FOR DETAILED STUDY." Translation: The other result samples didn't make any sense whatsoever, and we had locked ourselves out of the lab at 2 a.m. after we ingested all that psilocybin on mouldy whole wheat toastettes.

"TYPICAL RESULTS ARE SHOWN." Translation: We had to noodge the stats and this made the prettiest graph.

"SUBSEQUENT EXEGETICAL DATA MAY BE POSTED." Translation: I might get around to the ancillary studies being published, if you cheap tarts would fork over the Caruthers Enabling Grant for 2005.

"IN MY EXPERIENCE . . ." Translation: Once.

"IN CASE AFTER CASE . . ." Translation: Twice.

"IN A SERIES OF CASES . . ." Translation: Three times.

"IT IS BELIEVED THAT . . ." Translation: Looked okay to me, but I was totally stoned out of my gourd.

"IT IS GENERALLY BELIEVED THAT . . ." Translation: A couple of other white-coats standing with me beside the pop machine were high as Tim Leary in a Swiss toilet and they agreed to co-sign the fudged tally sheets.

"CORRECT WITHIN AN ORDER OF MAGNITUDE OF . . ." Translation: That is to say, wrong.

"ACCORDING TO STATISTICAL ANALYSIS . . ." Translation: Mrs. Grogan, the woman who cleans the lab at night, thinks it **might** encourage penile carcinomatous events if you rubbed it on your dick for 12 years.

"A STATISTICALLY ORIENTED PROJECTION OF THE SIGNIFICANCE OF THESE FINDINGS IS NOT AT PRESENT AVAILABLE." Translation: We fed Nutraphod to 17 Laplanders. Within a fortnight these hardy indigenes of the Northland turned cannibal and started fucking reindeer. The committee felt that the program as designed had perhaps begun to falter somewhat. Retrenching was spoken of, but then our Mission Operations Chief made the reluctant decision to set the Laplanders adrift off the Faeroe Islands in a spacious fiberglass dumpster with four days rations of Nutraphod and one reindeer.

"A CAREFUL ANALYSIS OF OBTAINABLE DATA . . ." Translation: Six notation binders detailing the metered readings of our four years of experimentation in pumping soda pop through the phloem of Brazil nut trees (*Bertholletia excelsa*) were by error left out for Salvation Army paper pickup and ended up in pillows donated to IOB, Incontinent Orphans of Bulgaria.

"IT IS CLEAR THAT MUCH ADDITIONAL WORK WILL BE REQUIRED BEFORE COMPLETE UNDERSTANDING OF THE PHENOMENON BECOMES PATENT." Translation: I haven't the foggiest, old boy. Don't understand a silly comma of it.

"AFTER ADDITIONAL STUDY BY MY COLLEAGUES . . ." Translation: The people working here with me in this environment, a chemistry laboratory engaged in technical calibrations requiring the gentlest of scientific touches, would be more suitably employed banging weight gongs at a circus. Last week I had to fire Lydia van Bezell when she repeatedly refused to suture the tapeworms unless Novocain was administered to them by painting it on with a small toothbrush. I explained over and over again that the Novocain was for us, the lab workers. Lydia is now an employee of the Toronto Planning Department where, happily for her, she has found her level of competence as a tailor sewing and fitting elf costumes to available legitimate dwarves each year before the Santa Claus Parade. Her future is not totally secure however, due to a growing prevalence of illegitimate dwarves showing up at Santa Claus Parade auditions.

"A HIGHLY SIGNIFICANT AREA FOR EXPLORATORY STUDY . . ." Translation: Another exquisitely useless topic selected by the moronic time-servers who comprise my committee. Last year the committee sat in solemn conclave (translation: got blasted out of their skulls at the Park Plaza Rooftop Bar) and approved a two-month study entitled "Brain-Breathing, Secret of the Aztecs: A

Physiometry of Oxygen Retention in South American Human Hair Follicles."

As Group Leader they selected a person known to the Canadian press as Steroid Stan, a disgraced Olympic tetherball champion with, however, a master of science degree. Before the university cancelled their appropriation, Stan and his cohorts had determined that the likeliest venue for their scientific undertaking would be Rio de Janeiro, preferably in February and March.

Upon rigorous investigation by the credentials subcommittee, we learned that Stan had received his master's degree from the South Nevada University of Duneology, at present operating from a mailbox address in Roadkillville, Arkansas. After due and serious deliberation, the committee felt that it could not in good conscience permit group leaders of subsidized projects to have obtained their postsecondary education primarily by submitting to their respective degree-granting institutions large numbers of Wheaties box tops.

"IT IS HOPED THAT OUR STUDY WILL STIMULATE FURTHER 1NVESTIGATION IN THIS FIELD." Translation: I quit, assholes! I've accepted the position of operations director for LORTZON, the comprehensive Argentinian ground squirrel count that begins this spring on Tierra del Fuego and then moves bravely northward. I will be taking up my new duties immediately upon my exit from the Betty Ford Center, 39000 Bob Hope Drive, Rancho Mirage, California.

THE 12 POLITICALLY CORRECT DAYS OF CANADIAN CHRISTMAS

On the 12th day of the Eurocentrically imposed midwinter festival, utterly oblivious of our Canadian aboriginal Moon of Cigarette-Smuggling Raven and indeed remembering not the coming Moon-of-Wolf-Who-Drives-Lexus-To-Whistler-After-Embezzling-Band-Funds, my Significant Other in a consenting adult, monogamous relationship gave to me . . .

12 males reclaiming their inner warrior through ritual scrotum-drumming

11 pipers piping (plus the 18-member contractually obligatory standby pit orchestra, made up of members in good standing of Canadian Musicians Equity necessary to be present although they may or will not be called upon to perform)

10 melanin-deprived, testosterone-poisoned scions of the patriarchal ruling class system leaping (possible clinical evidence of latah, the Malay Jumping Disease)

9 persons of the ninny persuasion engaged in rhythmic but goalless self-expression (or hapless victims of miryachit, the Siberian Jumping Disease, itself thought to be but a Slavic mirror of Latah)

8 economically disadvantaged female persons
purloining lactates from enslaved Bovine-Canadians

7 endangered swans swimming on federally
protected wetlands

6 enslaved Fowl-Canadians producing about-to-be-
filched ovoid reproductive structures

5 golden annular symbols of culturally sanctioned,
enforced domestic bonding,
(*Nota bene*: The calling birds, French hens, and
partridge have been seized by Environment Canada,
transported, and re-introduced into their native
habitat. Necessary revisions of the lyric ensue.)

4 purple Martins registered in Liberia for tax
purposes

3 French wens (all on the chin of ex-Premier
Landry of Quebec)

2 Turteltaubs, Avi and Sheila, both carrying Sierra
Club calendars printed on rolled afterbirth

and

1 Spotted Owl activist chained to an old-growth
pear tree

Merry Christmas!

1. At the department store, the gentleman in the red suit asks your Mommy, "How 'bout a little lap action for Santy?"

2. Santy's beard catches fire when he lights his pseudo-Dutch clay crack pipe.

3. Every few minutes Santy's beard rustles, and you hear a muffled meow.

4. Santy has to take a big suck on his bronchodilator puffer in between each "Ho" during the obligatory mirthful chortling.

5. During a pause in the interminable lineup of nasty, greedy, smelly children, Santy amuses the kids by demonstrating the "sleeper hold" on a Down's Syndrome elf.

6. The kids' letters to the North Pole are returned stamped "Addressee Unknown. Forwarded by government order to RCMP Office Investigating Fraudulent Mail Scams."

7. When young Deirdre climbs happily up into Santy's lap, his first words are, "Yank my beard, Tubby Little Girl, and I'll put the hurt on you."

8. On Christmas Eve, Santy finds a used nail in his Xmas shortbread cookie. Miffed, he pours his glass of milk all over Gran who is sleeping on the floor in the living room because she criticized Mom's pre-Christmas leg of lamb. All Gran said to her daughter was, "Most cooks remove the wool before roasting the leg. Been chomping on the Ecstasy again, you brainless slut?" Still really pissed about the nail that broke his dentures, Santy orders Donner to mount Blitzen and tells both of them to neigh loudly and moan a lot on the roof right in front of the bedroom window where the newlywed born-again cousins are wide awake at 3 a.m. still trying to figure out how to have sex through a hole in the IODE quilt so as not to see each other's naughty parts. When the newlyweds gaze out the bedroom window in horror at two male reindeer going at it for deer life on the roof, the couple fall out of bed on top of each other and accidentally discover fellatio.

9. On Christmas morning, young Gerald, who annoyed Santy at the mall, awakens in his bed to discover a freshly severed reindeer head under his blanket.

1. Monday, 4:45 p.m.

There I was in the very act of giving Grandmother Edith her vitally necessary, life-saving injection of heart medicine when the doorbell buzzed. Pushing Gran into the sewing-room broom closet so she wouldn't fall down, I ran to the door, flung it open, and was greeted by a girl of 14.

"My name is Deirdre Pestalozzi, sir. Would you like to sponsor me?" She smiled with the peach-warm glow of a Botticelli putto, and then continued, "Our school is having an uphill-rolling derby over at Sisyphus Park in support of the Canadian National Lophoanakyliosis Society."

"My, my, what a big word for such a little girl!" I said.

Deirdre shot back, "In other words, Wrinkly, you don't know what it means?"

"Well, er, that is. Okay. What is lophoanakyliosis? Sounds real bad."

"Well, it's no walk in the park, Pops. Let me say that right off the bat. It's the scourge of our nation, a black mark on Canadian goodness that we can let it continue without helping these poor people. My mom says you should cough up big-time, out of sheer guilt."

"Your mother has *quite a lot* to answer for."

"You in or out, Gramps?" Deirdre insisted.

Then I tossed in quickly, to throw her off balance,

"Who gets the money?"

"The poor, helpless lophoanakyliotics. Who do you think gets it? Santa Claus?"

"You mean," I said, pointing a prosecutorial finger at her, "there isn't a cent in it for you or your school?"

Deirdre sucked a finger tip and coyly curled a ringlet of her blonde locks, "Well, Mr. Man, you wouldn't begrudge a lonely little girl one trip to Fiji in a Lear Jet, would you? Mom says if we don't cure my hiccups, I could fail my best class: remedial baton-twirling."

"Gee willikers, when you put it like that, no one but an evil ogre could say no."

"So?"

"Fortunately for me, I have a small, basement-sized ogre to whom I offer board and room in my root cellar. I call on him for purposes of comparison such as these."

"And?" asked Deirdre.

"Why, my little sunbeam, he says, 'NO!'"

Deirdre seemed unpleasantly forward, but, when I tried to close my front door, I found her tiny foot had been placed firmly across the doorsill, so that, if I had slammed the door shut, I would have bisected little Deirdre's left foot.

The thought had undeniable appeal but I resisted it. Of late, the penalties for infantile vivisection are so harsh.

"Look, sweetie, I've got a very ill member of my family waiting in the sewing room for medical assistance." I pushed on the door to close it. But Deirdre wedged one elbow between the frame and the door. "If she's so sick, what's she doing in the sewing room? You got a sweatshop back there? You trying to get one more cheap dress finished before she croaks?"

"My grandmother's ongoing participation as certified union labour in the domestic garment industry is none of your business, young lady."

"Might be police business though, if it's granny exploitation." Young Deirdre frowned and a cloud passed over her face, not, however, a cloud toxic enough to terminate her babble. "Wow, I've heard of grinders of widows and orphans," Deirdre continued, "but, until this unwelcome day, I had never met one. Now, let's get serious, Father Time." Here Deirdre opened the door wide—rather boldly I thought, considering it was my door. "What can I put you down for?" For so dewy-fresh a moppet, Deirdre rubbed her little hands together in a veritable paroxysm of conspiratorial blackmailer's glee.

She repeated harshly, "So what can I put you down for?"

"Early retirement?" I said, being a bit of a card in my spare time. But the child was impervious to irony.

"Let's say forty dollars, okay?" offered Deirdre.

"Let's not." I knew my rights. "You still haven't told me what lophoanakyliosis is."

"It is a morbid desire to roll thalidomide babies uphill and then watch them careen downhill into heavy traffic."

"That's awful! I never heard of such a disease. Just one minute. I'm going to my library to check in the *DSM-IV*."

"Is that where you locked your sick grandmother?" whispered Deirdre.

"The *DSM* is the *Diagnostic and Statistical Manual of Mental Disorders* published by the American Psychiatric Association. If a particular lunacy is not listed there, then it is a highly suspect disorder indeed."

"*Au contraire*, Ancient of Days, some would say if a

disorder is listed there, then it is quite worthy of suspicion," sneered Deirdre, who was far too well informed for her age. "It is said that *DSM* writers are basically greedy shrinks who would pathologize every moment of daily life for the benefit not of patients but of American psychologists and psychiatrists—all this done at the dawn of a new millennium which generally looks askance at both the claims and the results of psychiatric snoopery."

I couldn't believe such eloquent but horror-laden deceit could pour forth from the mouth of a child. What were teachers getting up to these days? Actually teaching the young to question ordained authority? Why, there was no telling where it might end! Youth might begin to ask analytic questions about religion, about God, about our leaders! Dear me. And Deirdre looked so innocent and pert in her dark-blue school uniform: long skirt, blazer, and little school cap with the name sewn across the front: Blind Nuns of the Elora Gorge School for Girls. At best, a surprising and unusual scholastic venue for inquisitive young minds.

"Well, I'm sorry," I said. "Yes, it's dreadful behaviour. People who roll limbless children uphill ought to be spoken to quite sternly."

"But?" said Deirdre.

"But I have no intention of financing their rehabilitation."

"So you are going to pull a cheapo on me?" Deirdre looked disgusted.

"Yes." I said defiantly. "I'm as charitable as the next man."

Deirdre's eyes flashed. "Yeah, if the next man is Scrooge McDuck."

"Listen, Heidi, I have my limits, beyond which I will not be pushed. I am a friend to all of suffering humanity, day in and day out." Here I managed a sob and dabbed at my eyes.

"What's that noise back in the house?" Deirdre asked.

"It's Gran, trying to get out of the broom closet and find her heart medicine."

Finally I did succeed in slamming the door in her face. "And now, good day to you!"

2. Wednesday, 7 p.m.

The doorbell rings insistently. I open it to discover on the doorstep a cheerful lad of 13 carrying a clipboard and a felt pen. The boy has a large, official-looking badge on his windbreaker.

"Good evening, sir. My name is Rupert Poopert."

"Kid, I don't believe that name for a second."

"Would I make up such a spaz last name?"

"Possibly not. What are you collecting for?"

"Kyknothreptic Orphans of Ontario," said the boy quite forthrightly.

"And who are they when they are at home?"

"That's just the point. They have no home. They are orphans."

I nodded sagely, having just had Thanksgiving dinner. But I was through being fooled by bizarre charitable con games pulled on me by mere babes in the woods.

"What exactly is a kyknothreptic orphan?"

"It is a child abandoned by his or her parents near water in the environs of Stratford, Ontario, then found on the river bank and raised by swans."

"Kyknothreptic?"

"Yes," said the boy. "It is from two Greek roots and means literally 'nursed by swans.'"

"Where?"

"In the reed beds and mingled aquatic plants that line the shores of the Avon River."

"Good. Totally on the up-and-up. Then here, lad, take this cheque for three hundred dollars."

As the boy scampered happily down the front walk, I sighed aloud, "At last, a plausible charity."

We Canadians remain intrigued by the special uses to which the British sometimes put their gardens, uses that come to light in the pages of British tabloid newspapers.

A Season in a British Garden

MAY

Sharpen tools.
Plan to prune family tree.
Feed lime pit.

JUNE

Clear upstanding garden bones.
Cut back climbing aunt.
Drink plenty of lukewarm Bovril.

JULY

Poison Nigel's kipper.
Get Dad to inhale pesticide.
Disinter Mrs. Innis.
Bury Nigel near roses.

AUGUST

Feed cat to Dora.
Put Mrs. Innis under hydrangea.
Have a nice cup of tea.

SEPTEMBER

Set man-trap for milkman.
Purchase quick-dry cement.
Peek at Nigel to see if composting has begun.
Serve scones to police.

Today Hazel Delaney might be able to sell her aunt's trunk for two thousand dollars. Wow! There's a real TV show here in our little corner of Ontario. Boy! Cameras, quartz lights, RF microphones, coaxial cables, all strung hither and thither over the floor of the high school gymnasium. Look at those extender lenses on the TV cameras for those big closeups that viewers love. This is the most excitement we've ever had in Mutantville, Ontario.

I myself have been in line now since sun-up, here in the main corridor of the Mutantville High School. I have ticket number 35 and they've talked to 33 hopefuls, all of us lined up and lugging big packages, hoping for a windfall. Fiji, here we come. Why the host of the TV show, genial Dusty Progeriov, is so close I can smell his exquisite cologne, Old Ship Wreck. Enticing kind of an aroma, blending, as the label says, essence of lifeless bosun's mate with pleasantly rotting deck planks. Dry yet spicy too. Now we're getting some action. Yeah, here we go! The red lights on the cameras are lit and Dusty is actually interviewing guest number 34. It's Hazel Delaney. She's one of my neighbours and she brought an old flecked Belgian to be appraised. Dusty is checking it out now. He's lifting the cloth, palpating the Belgian in a professional manner, and—the moment we all pine for—delivering the price estimate. Jumpin' Jehosophat! Will you look at Hazel smile? Musta been a goodly ballpark figure to make Hazel beam like that.

Now it's my turn. The production assistants are motioning me to move forward briskly. Dusty is going to speak to me!

"Okey-dokey. Our next guest is Bill Crasselman. Where are you from, Bill?"

"Right here in Mutantville, Dusty."

"That's wonderful, Bill. Now let's take a gander at what appears to be a superb, late 20th-century, nicely waxed and polished alderman. These **are** rare! Let me just check the tissue tone and substance of this superb example. Hmmm. Where'd you pick this one up, Bill?"

"Well, actually, Dusty, I found it in a barn."

"Uh-huh."

"You won't find any scratches, missing parts, puck dents, or divots in that alderman, I can tell you that."

"Heh-heh. I'm sure we won't, Bill. Don't you worry. Now this is interesting, look here just under the collar by the neck piece of the alderman, you see that little mark, Bill?"

"Why, yes, yes I do see it, Dusty. What would that be?"

"That, sir, is a little thing we call the coroner's hallmark. See, after he has frisked a stiff, you know, made sure the bozo is defunct, as we like to say here on the *Antiques Shroud Show*, well sir, that coroner puts his mark on the corpse, usually with a broad-tipped indelible felt marker, a mark proving that he, the coroner, has examined said remains, and so now they can be put away, as this alderman obviously was, to mummy up and get nice and wizened, say, in the hay mow of a dry barn."

"Helps to preserve 'em, don't it?"

"Oh my, yes. You take a fresh one, all runny and oozy. You let it set out in the rain on a summer day, you're going to get droop. You're going to get incipient loss of structural integrity."

"What's that?"

"Oh, I don't know. Stiff's wig could fall off and get lost."

"Seen that a lot on a dead 'un."

"Sure you have, Bill. You don't preserve 'em right, you're going to get lock-arm and flap-jaw and fly-away-leg and popped-eyeball. All those minor flaws bring the price of an FP way down. By the way, Bill, we here at *Antiques Shroud Show* prefer you not to use the word *corpse*. Has a hint of death about it. We prefer the designation FP."

"Huh?"

"Former person. Keeps it respectful of the deceased entity."

"Well, we do want respect. Cost us all enough to keep these bodies stored for you people. We held fundraisers here in Mutantville."

"Did you, Bill? Tell me about that."

"Well, a lady across the street from me held a trousseau tea. Her daughter was getting married, so people from town showed up to gawk at the shower gifts and wedding presents. They pay a small fee and get to see the bride's new clothes, that's the actual trousseau, usually stored in the bride's hope chest."

"Sounds like fun. So what did you do?"

"Right after the trousseau tea, I had a torso tea. We raised money to keep the corpses safe at Nurtler's Cold Storage down by the river beside the old icehouse. Instead of a hope chest, I had the alderman stored in a dope chest."

"That's darn enterprising of you, Bill."

"Yeah, sure was, Dusty. Now what do you figure this alderman is worth? Sorry, this FP."

"Bill, you probably didn't know this. But aldermen and Rocky Mountain whistling marmots happen to be my cadaver specialties."

"I didn't know that, Dusty, and I'm a lesser man for it, okay? Now how much they gonna cough up for the stiff?"

"After consulting the missing-aldermen files at the Ontario Office of Potentially Deceased Worthies, I have determined that this is indeed one Pierpont Beresford Fleeb, who was, for a period of not less than four years, an alderman in Welland, Ontario. He disappeared on the night of March 23, 1999, while in the company of a Buffalo woman known to police as Tonawanda Wanda. Fleming vanished the same night that five forty-liter drums of pomegranate-scented baby oil went missing from Dubious Lubricants Limited of Thorold, Ontario. Alderman Fleeb and Wanda were last seen in the vicinity of a strip bar in Cheektowaga, New York, an establishment operating with a New York State liquor licence under the name of the "Polish Ballet Theater." No word of Alderman Fleeb has since been heard.

"So, Bill, I can say two things to you. One: this exquisitely preserved alderman will easily fetch five or six thousand dollars in the current no-longer-with-us market. Two: waiting to see you just off camera, in the earnest hope that you will be able to assist authorities with their inquiries, is Officer Lemuel Nurtler, commander of the Welland Constabulary's Special Squad, Operation Coffee Shop."

SEVEN REASONS ONTARIO & CANADA
WILL NOT JOIN THE U.S. IRAQ WAR

By Bill Casselman, war correspondent, *Atlantis Daily Bubble*

1. The sole, seaworthy Canadian Navy vessel, Rowboat HMS *Lewis MacKenzie*, is in use for early pickerel season on Lake Nipissing. We therefore have no means of troop transport to Iraq.

2. Innocent Quebec male might lose fingernail scratching ID off his conscription papers.

3. Ontarians too busy at home looking over their shoulders to see if they are on Stephen Harper's list of undesirables—this week's list, that is.

4. We don't need Iraqi oil. Ontario has its own oil supply. Isobel Bassett has agreed to donate Ernie Eves' hair to Exxon storage facilities.

5. Only limited potential sale of Canadian bacon in Iraq after the war.

6. Celine Dion can't sing to our troops due to
   exclusive Vegas contract.

7. Canadian Armed Forces needed at home in case
   of another snowstorm in Toronto.

From the driveway bulleting into our open kitchen window comes the yell, "They're baaaack!" Tiffany, our teen, iPod surgically sutured to her earlobe, spots a familiar car stop out front. Tiffany is quite advanced for 16. Although our daughter does not, for example, recognize paper money yet, she has learned that other people may exist and may not be mere products of her youthful imagination, as suggested by her deeper moments of solipsism. So now Tiffie does spare a nanosecond to inform her parents of the Freezers' arrival.

Usually Tiffie is not available to the outside world because she is listening intently to her latest favourite MP3 song. Today the Canadian rap artist known only as Bookless 'Sniff Yo Fish' Daddy Mimico-East Juvy-Prison Car-Wash is singing his latest hit, "Yo, I just offed a toddler on the TTC, didn't dig the all-day sucker she was wavin' at me."

We were expecting guests, of course. Awhile back Ben and Amanda Freezer, old friends since college, said they were going to pay us a visit soon. One small catch. They have arrived a year early. What college did we all attend? The Guelph Institute of Cheese-Mould Identification. What a fun seven years of intensive study we all spent there in the hallowed precincts of Wensleydale Hall! It's where Ben met Amanda.

"No matter what happens, we'll always have Paris," Ben Freezer likes to say.

"Yes," answers Amanda. "Paris, Ontario. And our thrilling discovery of that mutant Gorgonzola strain of mould on a forgotten sandwich in that charming little restaurant by the Grand River."

Ben usually chimes in at this point in Amanda's story, "We don't like to brag but at the time the Pasteur Medal was spoken of. Adrienne Clarkson telephoned and asked us personally to come to Rideau Hall and touch her cheeses. Amanda thought she had said 'Jesus' and that we had stumbled on some general-gubernatorial baptismal cult of Ottawa being performed on RCMP horses out in the Rideau Hall stables."

"Yes," sighs Ben, "I remember that little restaurant so well. That's where we first had *derzepnies.*"

"Oh?" Amanda has forgotten. "Just what were derzepnies?"

"It's the national dish of Tannu-Tuva, one of those autonomous republic thingy countries over on the Mongolian border with Russia."

"Well, I think now it's just plain Tuva. Derzepnies?

"Derzepnies are delicate little rolls of week-old porridge into which old men have sneezed."

Running at me wildly, Ben Freezer leaps from his still unbraked sedan screaming, "Billy, baby, booby, boy, haven't seen you in a coon's age!" Can this be so? Immediately I euthanize a raccoon and set to work on comparative time studies.

Ben and Amanda Freezer disembark from their lime Infiniti with their lemon children: Brillig, Slithy, and Tovah. An anthem of gratitude seems due. At once I begin skipping about the kitchen singing "O, Had I Jubal's Lyre," from Act 3 of Handel's oratorio *Joshua*. And a spirited rendition it is too, which not even sodium pentothal can quell. Loud enough to wake the Canaanites next door. Luella and Vern Canaanite? Surely you know them? Vern has two hardware stores in Oshawa. As Vern says sincerely, "Latex paint is my *life*."

Young Brillig Freezer is a mere 13 years old, his mother Amanda tells me.

"And no criminal record? Outstanding!" I say.

Brillig sneers, "Yeah, out standing in the rain, like you. What a total lame-o. Heard that one *in utero*, dude."

My, what an engaging child, I think, *and cognizant of Latin tags at his early age.* Quickly I send my wife to the garage to make sure there's a bag of fresh cement handy. Perhaps we have found a way to fill that small dry well in the backyard?

"So, you must be a real proud mom?" I go on, trying to encourage bonhomie.

"Eh?" replies Amanda, who is always quick on the uptake, especially if the uptake begins in a champagne flute. "Vern and I only like the good stuff, and we can afford it now. Know what I mean? The real vantage champagnes, like Dumb Chignon and Vulva Click-it."

Uneasily I grow aware of a high-pitched grinding sound issuing from some nether oubliette in the house. Dental drills awhirr are less foreboding. The noise seems to be coming from the basement. I hop down the cellar stairs to find young Brillig standing at our wet bar revving the Cuisinart as he drops my rare tropical fish, one by silvery one, into a foul froth of fish foam spuming up from the whirling death blades of the electric mixer.

Goodness, he has hold of Red Tide, my stud guppy! He's squeezing my guppy. Egad, the ruffian may induce premature milting. No! Don't drop him . . .!

Gone.

Sob.

My Cremesickle Molly! Squish.

My Abramite Head Stander! Mush.

My speckled Goby! Splorp!

Under the baleful fluorescence of my aquarium lights, orange shoals of glum koi flit and dither, alarmed at their friends' demise.

When I regain my composure, I ask Brillig, "Why would you do a thing like that, boy?"

"Because I was deprived of licorice as a toddler."

"Is that the poor wee guppies' fault?"

"Dude, somebody has to pay. Mom and Dad feed and clothe me, so I like to take it out on defenceless bystanders."

"What if I put your hands inside the electric blender?"

"It would be a daiquiri mix that would earn you three years less a day in the Kingston Penitentiary, where you would expand both your knowledge of prison life and your sphincters."

"Are you really only thirteen years old?" I ask.

"No. I'm a polymath dwarf stolen in infancy by gypsies from a University of Toronto experimental nursery. Look, I am merely attempting to ascertain which species of tropical fish disintegrate most quickly when subjected to a 'fatal stress event.' It's my grade eight science project for this spring."

"Cuisinarting a guppy is your idea of scientific inquiry?"

"Whadda ya want, dude? I could have taken the grant money and tried to save Quebec."

Of course, I never had great luck with tropicals. My kissing gourami fish usually tried to French one another and ended up ingesting their lovers whole.

I had better luck on a 1990 fishing trip near Huntsville when I purchased a bucket of live bait advertised as "old minnows." Indeed. Each minnow, due to prolongation of nutriment, had become a three kilogram carp. Naturally, I could not put a large carp on a hook as trout bait. But I took them home—poor little carplets—and found they made affectionate household pets. I taught the brighter carp to sing in unison the less tricky songs from Stephen Sondheim musicals and, as a concert ensemble named the Coral Choral, we toured Central Ontario gymnasia for several years, not without some failure.

Amanda Freezer suddenly clumps down the stairs and brays, "Are you men bonding like Crazee Glue?" At United Church Anti-Stridency Summer Camp Amanda's apt nickname was "Mack Truck."

"Bill, could I ask you the teensiest, weensiest favour? Would you and your wife and kids mind terribly moving into your garage for the two weeks that we're here as your guests?"

"What!"

Hubby Ben galumphs down the stairs now and waddles up to place a proud father's hand on the shoulder of his youngest guppycidal offspring. "Bill, it's like this. Amanda is very sensitive to noise."

"I have hyperacusis," sobs Amanda. "It's permanent."

Young Brillig holds up a box of facial tissues and passes them around.

"What is that in English, Amanda?"

"I have a pathologically acute sense of hearing."

Ben dabs a tear from his one good eye. Amanda ate his other one.

The precocious Billig adds, "It's a kind of auditory hyperesthesia in which the patient's hearing threshold is very low."

"I had no idea. I'm so sorry, Amanda."

Ben grabs his wife's hands in a gesture of support. Amanda slaps Ben in the face.

I continue, "What are the sounds, the noises, that most bother you, dear?"

"Other people breathing."

"Other people being alive," says her son. Ben slaps him. "Mom's pretty well your total, blister-packed fruit-cake."

"If you and your lovely wife and the kids could see your way clear to spending the next few days bunking out in your garage, I could get a real rest while I'm here." Amanda offers a plucky little smile. "You could make a kind of fun outing of it, no? A little holiday right at home. Campfire songs of yore. Weenie roasts. Remember those lovely old songs from summer camp sung in a circle as the bonfire burned low and the ruddy flames danced their reflection in the softly lapping lake waves?"

"And the campers nearest the bonfire were treated for first-degree burns?" added Brillig.

"To be honest, Amanda, I never went to camp. Had asthma." I say, trying to scuttle her fake enthusiasm as I summon up a cough.

Oblivious to my every word, Amanda burbles on, "Great old tunes! Don't you recall 'Gee, Mom, it's good we know/How I got impetigo.' Or 'Boy did I sing/squirm, when my roomie gave me ringworm.' If you lived in the garage you could have yoga classes in the morning, ritual scrotum-slapping in the afternoon, roasting Doctor Phil on a spit over a slow fire of an evening—whatever!"

"Gee, wouldn't that make a lot of noise and stir up your hyperacusis?" I venture.

With the airy flippancy of a dowager dismissing from service an impudent maid, Amanda waves off my concern. "It would make no more noise than ambulances whisking me back and forth to the emergency ward every day."

Ben and Brillig's eyes brighten oddly.

"So you agree? Super duper!" cried Amanda.

"One other thing, Bill?" says Ben.

"Yes?"

Ben goes on, "Could we beg you not to invite anyone else over to your house while we're here?"

Amanda blushes and puts a tentative finger to her lower lip. "I just hate to seem like a hypochondriac, Bill. But I'm allelophilophobic too!"

"Allelophilophobic? What's that?" I ask.

Brillig replies, "Mom breaks out in a rash if she thinks other people have friends."

"Well now, those modest strictures ought not to interfere with our family life too greatly. As I understand it: you want us to move out of our house into our garage for two weeks and not permit any other persons to enter the house while you, Ben, Brillig, Slithy, and Tovah live in our home? Is that it?"

"In a nutshell, yes." Amanda smiled.

So there's the answer. The way to handle house visitors

from Hell is to grant their every wish, to give in, to abase yourself at their feet cringing and fawning like the lick-spittle toady you are, in short, to fold like a cheap lawn chair. I hope then that this has cleared things up. I'd love to continue but I have to help my wife carry a new teak four-poster bed upstairs.

Our only neighbours out in the countryside are Lars and Morbulla Toivo. They are Finnish Baptists on Prozac. Fun couple. Lars and Morbulla have no children, but Morbulla has a pet elk named Sulk. Sulk the Elk is quite a raconteur and has brought many a Toivo party to a standstill with his rumbled imitation of Rudolph. Sulk got his name after an unfortunate incident during a local Santa Claus parade involving the elk's neck and a ten-year-old boy who the local paper described as "a husky lad." Weighing in at a feathery three hundred pounds, so he was.

Lars and Morbulla themselves are exciting conversationalists. After the initial thrill of stroking a live elk wears off for visitors (measurable tedium parameter: five to ten seconds), Morbulla has a nice line of anatomical quirks that she is only too happy to display for guests at the Toivo bungalow.

Says Morbulla cheerily to anyone who will listen, "See, most people with webbed feet have the webbing between all their toes, but I've got webs only between intermittent toes. My podal digital interstices are unique. Isn't that fascinating?"

"Why, Morbulla, you are positively pterodactyloid, my dear," said one of the guests who was far too well read.

As she bent down to remove a shoe to facilitate the display of her webbed feet, I said, "Uh, no, please don't show me. Morbulla, really, you don't have to take off your

Manolo Blahnik stiletto knockoffs. *Oh goodness, she took them off.* Yes, yes, I can see the little webs. Cute. That is interesting. *Please God, make her stop.*"

Morbulla natters on until visitors turn to pillars of salt. You know the saline transformation is completed when the Toivo cows sneak up, noodge you, and start licking your face. At that point Morbulla's husband Lars saves the party by explaining that he is an avid collector of nature's wonders. Lars has a quite comprehensive collection of collar linings for men's jackets. A whole new room out in the barn holds Lars's lifetime assemblage, with the collar linings neatly pinned to purple-felt mounting boards that lie inside tall glass cabinets arranged along one side of the barn. Lars will gladly show you the full richness of his gathered treasures: light, flexible collar linings for spring jackets, even-lighter collar linings for summer, heavier and sturdier collar linings for winter jackets, and then, excitingly, back again to light collar linings for spring jackets. And yet only twice after a "collar tour" has Lars been wounded by gunshots fired by party guests.

At the Toivo's chic summertime soirees, weather and supply of antidepressants permitting, guests are encouraged to frolic on the spacious lawn that encircles the elk's "slopping pond." "Sulk is just our little water baby," coos Morbulla, chucking the elk under its chin. Often the playful Sulk will snap at Morbulla's fingers. But so far she has only lost a tiny piece of one cheek.

When the guests all gather around the pond where Sulk mopes, Morbulla pipes up brightly, "Our little Sulk has a sweet tooth for bot-fly larvae, don't you, Elky-Welky? So Lars and I keep a few dead things in the mudroom. When Sulk is in the dumps, a nice scoop of maggots plump from feasting on fresh roadkill peps our little elk right up."

Only the trusted visitor is allowed to view the inner sanctum, the room at the back of the barn. In what used to be a stall for a plough horse, Lars keeps the objects of his special hobby. Lars knows that most people would not be able to understand a grown man with Canada's largest collection of Judy LaMarsh dolls.

If even that exquisite rarity fails to interest visitors, Morbulla steps right up. "Did I ever tell you that I have an episiotomy scar shaped exactly like Prince Edward Island?"

"Oh I hope not," whines the hapless guest, backing slowly towards the side door of the barn and thinking, *Is it rude if I actually run away from her?*

When visitors eyes glaze over like Ming vases, introduced next will be the Toivos' marital-sex anecdotes, always a polite topic to share at dinner: "So I said to Lars at that very moment, 'Oh, put it away, Lars. I'd rather do it with a walrus.' And Lars—he's such a card—said, 'Vel, Morby, perhaps I vil iust arrange for dat.'"

Should you be caught in the roadkill mudroom observing the maggots consume the squished raccoon and suddenly find your chin flopping downward into your chest, Morbulla will tiptoe up behind you and whisper, "My cousin Fred is a frogman."

"What? Oh? Professional diver, eh?"

"No. I'm afraid with Fred, it's genetic," she explains.

"Ewww."

"Oh yes. Our family doesn't like to talk about it." Here Morbulla leans into your face and rasps, "Fred breathes through his skin. In the winter Fred fills his swimming pool with mud and hibernates out there for months."

"Must be tricky for his wife? Been together a long time, have they?"

"They're a team now."

"Lotsa things in common, eh?"

"Well, she has webbed feet too!" says Morbulla, beaming. "And you should see Fred's children! Their inclusion on the endangered amphibians list has been spoken of favourably."

But luckily by now you have reached your vehicle. When you thank Lars and Morbulla for a really, truly, lovely, lovely evening, Lars remembers an interesting scrap of American history. As you accelerate your SUV briskly, the last thing you hear is the sound of Lars Toivo's incessant drone: "A lot of people, they do not know that the American clergyman Cotton Mather lived from 1663 to 1728, yes? Vel, Cotton Mather had a lesser-known Puritan uncle named Fecal Mather."

"Bye! Bye!" screams Morbulla.

Lars turns to his wife, "Morbulla, did they turn back towards us for the traditional valedictory wave from a departing automobile? Do you think they could not hear me perhaps? Morbulla? Oh my very goodness! Morbulla, don't do that to an elk!"

"Awesome news, dude."

"What?" I said.

"We're going to die."

"Bummer. When?" I asked Nigel, our photographer.

"Oh, in about one minute," said Nigel.

Aluminum screamed. Rivets shrieked, protesting their enclosure in metal plates. Verna, our production assistant, knelt in the aisle of the airplane and began to pray, "Like, Mr. God, please let me live. Geez, I haven't even had a chance to try blotter acid yet." The airplane careened into a loopy parody of descent that might have alarmed even experienced old descenders like Dante and Virgil.

We were 32,000 feet above the Caspian Sea, a few minutes past Baku, oil city of Azerbaijan, flying to the tiny country of Halooshistan, a green patch on the brown quilt of Central Asia, a rare surviving khanate where Nog, Eternal Khan of Halooshistan, held sway over winds that rippled mountain grasses and swept groves of Halooshi pine. The population of the khanate, even by the meagre measure of surrounding countries, was picayune. One hundred and twelve thousand Halooshis throve on the high green plain of Wouz, and gazed down upon their perpetually warring neighbours with bemusement and genuine confusion.

The Khan was a Harvard graduate, *magna cum laude*, a master of arts in Comparative Linguistics. Nog Khan had titled his successfully defended thesis "A Comparative Burial Vocabulary of Old Scandinavian and Homeric Greek." His nickname at Harvard had been "Eggnog."

My editor at *The Daily NeoCon Job* wanted a travel piece on the smeeb harvest. "And, Billy Boy, you are just the naïve yokel for this assignment. How do I know? You are twenty-four years old, have no living relatives and you are desperate for your first byline. This could be it."

Our airplane's wings grew sick of cleaving air. They began bucking to thwart the laws of aerodynamics. Ailerons on the edges of wings flipped and flapped, neglectful of their aerofoil duty. One wants wings to be uppity, of course, but to remain at all times good sports about the whole flying business. One of my less pushy internal organs, heretofore unknown to my proprioceptive sense, suddenly presented itself at the back of my throat and began to insist on being deposited in my lap.

"I will never fake an orgasm again," prayed Verna.

Our flight to little Halooshistan had not begun urgently. We had pooled reporters to obtain a planeload of news guys and features gals and we were sharing the rented plane with two other newspapers and a wire service.

Over the banshee wail of engines came the pilot's cracking voice on the PA, "When we are upon land, please you to run most speedily to the airport building. Do not look around, gentlemens. Do not linger to void distended urinary bladders upon our sacred shrines, some of which border the runways. I know you infidels of the West. Always pissing out your waters on what is foreign."

The pilot peeked out through the open cockpit door, nodded frantically and said, "When feet are on land, accelerate most spiritedly in your onrush to the haven of our spacious airport lounge."

The plane lurched through the sky. We felt the automatic pilot kick in. Like a ghost the pilot loomed up in the little cockpit doorway. Shaken and pale, he wobbled down the aisle carrying a tureen of glutinous broth from which he ladled individual servings into foam-plastic cups. As it seemed mere seconds before we might smithereen on a mountainside or plunge screaming into the greedy billows of the Caspian Sea, it was perhaps an odd moment to serve the evening meal. But dine we did, there and then. "No cutlery," he intoned sadly. "Is soup. Please to suck it orally into the unsewn mouth cavity." Yes, the pilot had learned English from an embalming manual.

Nigel Pinguidy, our Cornish photographer, glugged down the thick broth and pronounced it "a toothsome in-flight feast of unidentified hooves and corn husk leavings."

An hour later, in ten testicle-retracting seconds, the airplane dropped 50 feet and we landed safely.

Halooshistan is a small country, green but poor. How poor? So poor there is only one Halooshi surname. Everyone in the country is named Oduts. Say it with equal stress on each syllable, to rhyme with "Oh. Nuts."

The government translator and guide who met us at Oduts International Airport was Nognur Oduts.

His brother, who drove the '62 Plymouth taxi that took us to the Imperial Oduts Hotel, was Nurnog.

I bet you think their father's first name was Nugnor?

Well, it wasn't, Smarty-pants.

Their father's given name was Odutsi.

Nugnor was their uncle.

Nornug, their most gracious auntie, offered the whole crew cold lemonade that hot afternoon on her veranda overlooking the smeeb plantation. Smeeb is an exotic local fruit whose pulp is dried and fluffed to make lint for spotless houses. Okay, I jest. But smeeb lint is used throughout Halooshistan to stuff pillows, sofas, armchairs, and dead relatives. Auntie Nornug confessed with a giggle that she had spiked our lemonade with fermented smeeb hearts. Quite yummy.

Smeeb harvesting is simplicity itself. When the fruit is ready, when the tender smeebs are swathed in downy, pubescent fuzz, often by mid-January, the fruits develop an uncanny ability to detect the approach of humans. And so in the deep of the night Halooshi smeeb-harvesters, wearing special sandals wrapped in cushions, tiptoe up to the squat little bushes heavy with moist smeebs and shout something very much like "Boo!" The poor, startled smeebs go into a kind of fruit-tree dither. They get all excited and lose control of their stems. A chemical reaction induces the absciss layer, special cells involved in leaf-fall and stem-break, to drop the fruit to the ground. There the fruits dehisce with a farty ripping sound, and as they split, the smeebs turn into giant balls of easily plucked fluff. Not unlike Canadian voters when a writ is dropped, I thought.

The smeeb plantation where we dined lay on the outskirts of Bughur, the capital of Halooshistan. As the Halooshistani ambassador to Canada always insists, his voice rising towards the rafters of hysteria, the word is an iamb, metrically short–long. "One must *never* stress the first syllable of our capital. It is the second syllable that is stressed." When Dr. Oduts makes this pronouncement he always stamps his foot manfully. The force of his protest is diminished only slightly when hearers spot his slippers with the purple sequins.

Getting there: If you're planning a fun getaway to the smeeb harvest, Airoflop flies DC7s twice yearly on direct flights to Halooshistan from Mutantville Airport near Toronto. Return starts at $980 CDN. Accommodations in Bughur are limited to Ali's See-Through Glass Motel for Infidels, a perfectly secure pied-à-terre on the outskirts of town, nestled in a historic tar pit. Watch dinosaur ribs bob playfully to the black water's surface as you attempt sleep. Outside, a haunting serenade helps summon Morpheus as a giant choir wends towards the temple of NogNog singing the traditional hymn of praise for the popping of the smeebs. Many countries feature massed choirs. In Halooshistan it's a masked choir.

PART 2
Words in My Life

A word nut's canoe can get tippy too, piled high as it sometimes is with verbal cargo. As my word canoe tips, I generally head for the keyboard and make for shore by tapping out a bit of word lore. These are recent pieces that resulted from such sessions. I trust you will enjoy the reading as much as I did the writing.

I particularly hope you'll have time to read one of my own favourite pieces in this collection. It's the last essay in the book. It's called "A Risley Act: A Real Term in Showbiz Slang" and describes the best laugh I ever had in my life.

The Pedantry Shelf or Who Let the Lesser Omentum Out of Its Cage?

In my quest for verbal oddments I chanced recently upon a delectable collection of medical words. These have fascinated me since the day I discovered that fungosity meant "a small, soft wart." I have used that word often at parties and have found it a stimulant to conversation that no one should be without. In fact, I have brought many a party to a complete standstill by wandering about the room pointing out selected words and photographs in old surgical textbooks. Is that why partygoers shun me? I just don't know why people don't take to me at parties.

Medicine abounds in exotic verbiage. The only word in the English language with three contiguous *o*'s belongs to the doctors. In sesquipedalian splendour it rejoices in being that long-winded operation hysteroöophorectomy. By the time the patient has managed to pronounce it, it's over.

The lesser omentum could be a furry wee beast of the raccoon ilk. Actually it is the double fold passing from the lesser curvature of the stomach to the transverse fissure of the liver. But it's all yours.

There is a part of your mortal shell called by the official New Latin medical but horrific appellation: *iter a tertio ad quartum ventriculum*. This is also an old Roman recipe for porridge.

Each of us possesses an arachnoid foramen. Someone will say, "I use to know an Outer Mongolian milkmaid in

Toronto by that name. She had a lovely personality. Liked to pull on your ears, though, in an insistent manner that could be off-putting depending on the time of day. She preferred early morning." The said foramen, however, is an opening in the roof of the fourth ventricle of the brain. It has specific survival motor functions. It helps humans click a TV remote whenever they identify reruns of programs featuring Jerry Lewis.

What unknown menace lurks in Henke's retrovisceral space? Is Henke there? Was he ever? Have they evicted Henke and converted the space to a condo? Is Jerry Lewis doing the telethon?

Each hippocamp in us has its own fimbria. They are very happy together, I'm told, and are planning a June wedding.

Then we all have Fraenkel's Glands. But what about poor Fraenkel? Things can get pretty sticky for a man without glands.

As for Froriep's (pronounced Smith) Ganglion, I say give it back to Froriep (pronounced Jones).

Cowering silently within us all is Grymfelt's Triangle. There is no mention whatsoever of his rectangle. I hope it's working properly. A plugged rectangle plays havoc with one's plumbing.

There exists Haller's ansa. But who asked the pushy bastard in the first place?

At times we may all have Hesselback's hernia, Heryng's benign ulcer, Kussmaul's coma, Zinn's zonula, Lietaud's sinus, Mildred's ear and Uncle Fred's shoulder blade, though I should hope not all at the same time.

Onychophagy afflicts vast multitudes in Canada. In fact, there ought to be a Christian Women's League against it by now. This is the medical word, based on two Greek roots, for biting the fingernails.

Perhaps the most bizarre verb of my acquaintance is hepatize. And I've met some pretty weird verbs up dark alleys, let me tell you. Okay, okay, maybe I'll tell you another time. To hepatize is to change something into liver. It is related, you can see, to the word *hepatitis*; and it gave rise to a novella I wrote entitled "The Unfortunate Hepatization of Mike Harris." I had intended it to be a horror story. But it failed. I forgot that to be changed into Mike Harris is a fate worse than liver.

Hair in the armpit is called hircus. So the next time you have occasion to address in a formal manner Mike Harris's armpit you may begin, "O Hircus, when thy fetid . . . er . . . fêted."

Take this sentence: "He palpebrated at her." Call the OPP! Doesn't it sound obscene? It means merely 'He winked at her.'

He's a pygalgia. Pygalgia means 'a pain in the buttocks.' This could be an excellent code word to identify unsavoury office layabouts without giving immediate offence.

The possibilities are endless, but this article is not. I must lay down my quill now, or I may suffer a prolapsed axilla. That's a fallen armpit to you, fellah! And it can be pretty ugly. But then so was Mike Harris as premier of Ontario. It is rumoured that Jerry Lewis is going to play Mike Harris in an upcoming CBC drama series "The Common, Senseless Revolution."

Avril Lavigne is a young Canadian superstar songstress whose voice and clever stage persona I enjoy. In performance Lavigne both gives herself to and withholds herself from the audience, in a most tantalizing mode of musical presentation. Her surname intrigued me and if names interest you, you'll find what I dug up fascinating.

We begin with two negatives. This is NOT genealogy. This is NOT necessarily the origin of Avril Lavigne's family name. This is the origin of the French family name *Lavigne* as it may have occurred with some families. It might be valid for Avril's family. It might not be.

French onomastics is a complex study. There are few certainties and masses of exceptions. But here are some of the things we know.

There are two common origins of the French surname Lavigne. *La vigne* is the French word for 'vineyard,' land where grape vines are planted. The word *vigne* appears in French by 1120 CE. It derives from Latin *vinea*, the word that Cicero, Horace, Vergil, and Plautus all used for vineyard. The Roman poet Horace was particularly fond of the word and no doubt of what vineyards produced.

Vinea is itself from Latin *vinum* 'wine.' But our English word wine does not derive from the Latin *vinum*, as some will say. English *wine* and Latin *vinum* and Greek *oinos* are cognates, literally words 'born together,' but technically the three words descend separately from the same Indo-European root. Indo-European is the ancient, unwritten language that is the mother of hundreds of modern languages. From the Greek word for wine, English made the fancy term for the study of wine and wine-making, *oenology*.

Lavigne began as a byname, a *dit* name in French, to designate one who owned a vineyard. *Dit* is the past participle of the French verb *dire*; it means 'called' or 'named.'

The first appearance of the name Lavigne in French wills and parish registers is usually in a form like this: *né, fils de Pierre le Gros dit Lavigne* 'born, a son to Big Pete called The Vineyard.' This implies that this parish held two or more Big Petes. One way to differentiate among them was to add a descriptive about where one lived or what the other owned. In the quoted register entry recording the birth of his son, this Big Peter is identified as one who grew grapes and probably owned his own vineyard. Sometimes within even two or three generations of the beginning of the name, the family would pick the *dit* name as their legal surname, Lavigne. In other cases the family would take the ancestor's nickname and become legally *la famille Le Gros*.

Other early entries recording births, deaths, and inheritance of property were written like this: *Marcel de la vigne* 'of the vineyard' may have been the Marcel in that parish who worked picking grapes or making wine. Another recorded early form is *Thierry La Vigne* 'Thierry the Vineyard' is likely to have owned such land. By omitting the French preposition *de*, the monk meant to make the locative "*La Vigne*" pointed, demonstrative. Thierry was "the vineyard" because he owned it. This early practice was the very opposite of later French naming tricks where *de* was added to make ordinary names sound aristocratic. So later Germans added von and Dutch speakers added *van* to outsnoot their neighbours.

Bynames

What is a byname? Here's another take. Glen Fisher and Leslie A. Schweitzer in a 1992 article give this apt introduction:

> Most names before AD 1600 have two parts, a given name and a byname. A given name is a personal name (such as Caitlin, Rhys, Wulfric, or Elizabeth) which your parents would give you. We don't call it a first name because it doesn't always come first. In Hungarian, for instance, the bynames come first, before the given name. Bynames originally distinguished between people with the same given name. Anything that could be used to tell two people apart could be used as a byname. For example, a large English town in the 13th century might have had Roger Baker (who baked bread for a living), Roger Johnson (whose father was names John), Roger Bigge (who was notably large), Roger Bywater (who lived by the river), and Roger London (who once lived in London).
>
> Bynames were usually short, direct, earthy, and concrete, rather than long and fanciful; after all, they were used every day. As well, they were usually bestowed upon someone, and not chosen by them. One wouldn't be Robert the Philosophical Poet, but Robert Talkewell (who talks well), or, worse, Robert Boast.

Originally, children acquired bynames of their own, different from their parents' (so John Baker's son might be Thomas Johnson). Later some bynames became inherited surnames, as we have today, so Thomas Johnson's father might really be named Paul, and Edward Baker might actually be a goldsmith.

Middle names, as we use them today, didn't exist; most names had just a given name and a byname. The exceptions usually added a second byname to an inherited surname. For example, Nicholas Osbourne the blacksmith would be named Nicholas Osbourne the smith to distinguish him from Nicholas Osbourne the potter. [Note from B.C.: And in the next generation the legal surnames of their sons could become Nicholas Smith and Nicholas Potter.]

Next come Lavigne surnames based on the village or town in which the ancestor lived. There are dozens and dozens of hamlets, towns, hills, crossroads, and whistle-stop places in France called Lavigne. At first there were only first or given names. Then, as European populations increased and as people began to have property to leave to their relatives, it became important to know which precise Pierre was referred to in a will or other legal document. So, in a small town named Lavigne, there might have been two or three men with a very common name like Pierre. To make certain of preventing confusion among them, extra little words or nicknames were added to Pierre. That, in a simplified explanation, is how most last names began. Pierre Lavigne was Pierre from the town of Lavigne, whereas the other Pierre in town was a big man. His nickname became his legal surname: Pierre Le Gros.

Lavigne was a common substitute spelling used by French Jews whose previous surname forms might have been Lévi, Lévine, Leven, Laveen, Levien, Leviene, Levigne, Le Vine, La Vine, and even Lhévinne. A variety of motives spurred such name changes. Often a Russian Jewish immigrant to France named Levin became Lavigne simply to make the name appear more French. Sometimes anti-Semitism, both legal and illegal, forced Jews to try to "blend in." Other families looked upon the name change as a mere orthographical variant.

As an ancient Hebrew given name, Levi signifies Levitic descent, that is, supposedly direct in line from Levi, third of the 12 sons of Jacob, and so of the tribe of Levi, one of the 12 tribes of ancient Israel. Formerly (but with a diminished role today) the Levites assisted priests in worship. They were custodians of the Tabernacle, the so-called bodyguards of God, for Levites carried the Ark of the Covenant in holy procession. The section of the Christian Bible called Leviticus, containing details of laws and minutiae of Jewish ritual is a shortening of its name in Latin, *Liber Leviticus* "the book of the Levites."

More on French-Canadian *Dit* Names

Here is an extract from one French-Canadian genealogical study, presented to give the reader an idea of the tricky convolutions of French surnames. This passage was translated from French, but not by me.

In the earliest documents of Trois-Rivières, dating back to 1651, Nicolas Rivard was referred to with the title "Sieur de la Vigne." Nicolas, oldest son of Pierre Rivard, was the first of the family to arrive in New

France in 1648. Nicolas's mother, Jeanne Mullard, owned a small piece of land in Tourouvre, named Clos de LaVigne. This LaVigne location exits in Tourouvre to this day, where one of our cousins visited and kindly provided us with a picture of a local road sign. Nicolas' oldest son Nicolas and youngest son Antoine also used the *dit* name LaVigne, but the *dit* name was not routinely used after the first three generations. While most families in this line retained Rivard, we have recently discovered numerous families in Quebec that dropped Rivard and kept Lavigne as the surname. Many of the Lavigne families were from the Nicolet area.

Following is a passage about the use of *dit* surnames in Quebec. I have lost the name of the author, but will cheerfully add it, if any reader can identify this text. By presenting this snippet, I do not indicate that I agree with all this author's statements and conclusions:

French Canadians are descended from a relatively small number of immigrants. On top of that, many names were homonyms. The result is that the number of family names in French Quebec today is very small (a few thousand) compared to that in France (hundreds of thousands). Everything was determined in the early centuries of settlement.

The distribution of the most common family names of baptized individuals before 1800 shows that 37 family names accounted for more than 1,000 baptisms, 150 for more than 500, and 962 for more than 100. The 15 most common names were used by more than 28,000 individuals, and 1,400 names covered almost 95% of all individuals born in the colony before 1800.

. . .

A *dit* name is an alias given to a family name. Compared to other aliases or a.k.a.'s given to one specific person, the dit names were given to many persons. It seems the usage exists almost only in France, New France and in Scotland where we find clans or septs. [Note from B.C.: Not true. Bynames are a part of surname history for many, many peoples and languages of the earth.]

Many of the soldiers of the Carignan Regiment who came here in 1665–1668, lived around Dauphine. While they were not the only ones or the first to use *dit* names in New France, it seems those soldiers are responsible to a great extent for *dit* names reaching Quebec. This would explain, for example, why there is a concentration of families with *dit* names around Lac St-Pierre. There seigneuries belonged often to retired officers from the Carignan regiment.

One of the most important words in anyone's life is their surname. Before your canoe tips, it is good to know how you were labelled during your earthly voyage. Every name has a story to tell, and these stories were what I found while listening to Avril Lavigne, *chanteuse extraordinaire*, sing. I offer them to you and to her.

Next, our canoe tips at the comic scene of the naming of the Confederation Bridge to Prince Edward Island.

What a corny, frumpish name! Confederation Bridge. Isn't that dreadful? Another Waspy, bureaucratic bit of toponymic tedium from Ottawa. Another yawn of a Canadian name to dull the cartographical expanses of Canadian mappery, bland as some of it already is with boring place names. Did you know that Queen Victoria's name appears more than three hundred times on Canadian maps? Give us a break!

Many citizen voters in PEI and New Brunswick wanted the bridge to bear a distinctively Canadian Maritime name, 'The Abegweit Crossing.' The word is pronounced EPP-eh-kwit, all syllables short. For ten thousand years Abegweit has been the affectionate way Mi'kmaq people refer to Prince Edward Island. Loosely translated from the Mi'kmaq language, Abegweit means 'cradled on the waves.' More precisely, the Mi'kmaq root is *epegweit*, 'lying in the water,' or *abahquit*, 'lying parallel with the waves.'

The first humans who came to the island were Mi'kmaq hunters. They paddled to Abegweit even in the wintertime by canoe to fish and take wild fowl; and after drying their catch along the shores of Bedeque Bay, they would return to permanent winter camp on the nearby mainland.

The Mi'kmaq divided their ancestral lands into seven parts, which still bear the ancient names, as attested in the Mi'kmaq Grand Council for the District of Epekwitk (Abegweit). Most people who have called the island home have been more than fond of this lovely, watery name.

Here is Lucy Maud Montgomery, author of *Anne of Green Gables*, writing in 1939 in Prince Edward Island: "You never know what peace is until you walk on the shores or in the fields or along the winding red roads of Abegweit on a summer twilight when the dew is falling and the old, old stars are peeping out and the sea keeps its nightly tryst with the little land it loves."

Ships have proudly born the name of Abegweit. A CNR automobile ferry that used to ply the waters of the Northumberland Strait between New Brunswick and PEI was christened MV *Abegweit*. Then in 1962, the body of water crossed by the ferry was officially named Abegweit Passage. Since the new bridge straddles this part of the Strait, Abegweit Crossing is logical as well as resonant of history.

Samuel de Champlain called Prince Edward Island Île de Saint Jean in 1604. The British possession of the island in 1759 caused a simple translation to St. John's Island. Then in 1798 the British garrison at Halifax was being commanded by Prince Edward, Duke of Kent, and some local royalist, some cringing, lickspittle toady, thought it might be kiss-assy to name yet another piece of colonial real estate after yet another imperial poobah. That Prince

Edward, the island's namesake, was the father of Queen Victoria.

So why has some glum mugwump in Ottawa named this structure Confederation Bridge? Are federal bully-boys reminding Islanders of how much they owe to Confederation, a reminder all the more piquant to Ottawa politicians in this year of a possible federal election? You betcha!

Elsewhere in Canada, enlightened officials are not abandoning native names like Abegweit. They are doing just the opposite. They are returning aboriginal place-names to our maps. The community of Frobisher Bay now bears its prime Inuit name, Iqaluit.

At his home on Prince Edward Island, I telephoned John Joe Sark, hereditary captain of the Mi'kmaq Grand Council for the District of Epekwitk (Abegweit). In spite of the announcement that Confederation Bridge was the name, Mr. Sark was in cheerful fettle, busy making plans for an alternative naming ceremony to which he is going to invite leaders of first peoples from across Canada. "What name are you going to use to consecrate the bridge?" I asked. "Abegweit!" laughed John Joe.

Stompin' Tom Connors, as his fans might expect, includes a song on his album *The Confederation Bridge* detailing the meaning of Abegweit and some of the word's history.

At the end of May, official celebrations to open the bridge will, of course, include a visit by Prime Minister Chrétien and assorted high muckamucks. Oh, the officials will be careful to invite a few Mi'kmaq people. But not wanted at the party will be their word, Abegweit.

Shame on an Ottawa deaf to history, deaf to the oldest human sounds to have echoed across this land, and deaf to those who hold Abegweit in their hearts, where it is a word as warm as home.

Note: From 1995 to 1998 Canadian Geographic *magazine published a bimonthly column by me entitled "Our Home & Native Tongue" in which I examined the treasures of Canadian English as they related to our place-names and geography. This column appeared in the March-April 1997 issue of* Canadian Geographic.

The modern English word *Easter* derives directly from
the Old English or Anglo-Saxon word *Eastre* or *Eostre*.
The Angles, the Saxons, and the Jutes had no dictionary
to standardize spelling and so orthographical variation
ran wild, much as Eostre did, sporting nymphlike
through the woodlands of spring.

Contrary to what you may peruse in many modern
dictionaries, there is no proof whatsoever, not one iota of
historical evidence, that Eostre was a goddess of dawn.
We have no surviving image of Eostre in all the lovingly
museumed depictions of ancient British, Celtic, or
European deities.

What we know with certainty is that the Christian
Easter celebration took its name from *Eostur-monath*, the
Anglo-Saxon word for the month of April, literally
Eostre-month.

Older etymologies say that her name originated in
Old Teutonic, from **austrôn-* 'dawn.' The laws of vowel
and consonant change and derivation do not permit such
an origin. **Austrôn* cannot evolve into Eostre. At least it
has not happened so far—here on earth. That etymology,
widely printed in major English dictionaries, is wrong.

Then who was this coy and modest goddess? The
modern, questing etymologist looks at the Classical
Greek word *oistros*, not for an origin, but for a cognate,

that is, a word born from the same Indo-European root as Eostre. Now that derivation does obey the laws of verbal cognateness.

Oistros was a large European horsefly whose painful bite drew blood and caused cattle to run wild, even stampede. The insect's Victorian zoological name was *Tabanus bovinus*, where *tabanus* is the Latin word for horsefly or gadfly. Today Oestrus is the genus name of the common botfly, a similarly nasty little insect whose larvae are parasites in mammal tissues and body cavities, mammals such as humans, horses, and cows.

We know the Greek word in more familiar dress as *oestrus* or *estrus*, its Latin forms. In modern physiology estrus is the female equivalent of the word *rut*. When a female animal is "in heat" it is in estrus. In Classical Greek *oistros* meant 'frenzy,' 'sexual rage,' 'ravening, slavering female lust.' It described the scary maenads, drunken women running wild over the Greek mountains, spring-moon-mad in their ecstatic worship of Dionysus, futtering the night away in unholy orgies of forbidden lust, catching a male "chase animal," ripping his body apart, and devouring him in oozing gobbets of flesh. Hey, girl, beats a slow bowling night!

The Greeks thought you could catch such sexual ardour from being bitten by a gadfly. *Oistros* meant 'gadfly' too. More to the point, Herodotus (*Histories* ch.93.1) uses *oistros* to describe the desire of fish to spawn. So its root meaning is probably 'rage' with a later semantic overlay of 'raging, powerful sexual urge.'

That's something pagan peoples celebrated every spring, the upsurge of sap in tree and plant and human.

The Anglo-Saxons *Eosturmonath* was Sex Surge Month, not as dainty as April perhaps, but much more to the pagan point.

Hey, Boadicea, let's rut!

Keep all this in mind and in hand at Easter service.

What odd tie binds the medical word ptosis *and the bird word* ptarmigan? *Only this brief essay can answer that riveting question.*

Willow Ptarmigan I judge to be an apt name for a maiden in a fantasy novel. An all-Canadian hero meets her while trundling his hoopla over the tundra. She's a comely lass, who coos and gurgles and croaks as she tugs you down into the vulval warmth of her feathery snuggery. Her nest I mean—of course! Willow P. might also meet our hero in the midst of a boating lesson on a lake in Algonquin Park, as their canoe tips. She's giving him canoe lessons and it begins badly. But it ends well because he admires her feet, not as a fetishist, but because hers are major-league trotters, *pieds* displaying podal symmetry of delirious proportion.

Back in bird-world, the ptarmigan's fluffy winter feet are appealing. So cute were the ptarmigan's feathered tootsies that zoologists gave one species the name *Lagopus lagopus,* based on two Greek roots that mean 'rabbit foot' in direct reference to the bird's feet that seemed to early scientific examiners rather like the furry feet of an Arctic hare.

The initial *p* of ptarmigan is quite false, a spurious addendum by a meddlesome lackwit, for the original word was *tarmigan.* During Victorian times—when else?—there was a mania for correcting English spellings.

Thus misguided, semiliterate fussbudgets galumphed through our word stock adding and subtracting letters with ignorant abandon. For example, the letter *s* in the word *island* is an ignorant infix. Island does not come from the Latin word *insula* 'island' but from the Old Norse word *igland*.

The same faltering twits thought sure that ptarmigan must be Greek, and have an initial letter *p* that was silent, as in pterodactyl, ptomaine poisoning, Ptolemy, and ptosis.

How did it happen? It's the fault of a once-used but now obsolete medical word *ptarmic*. In the 17th century a ptarmic was a specific used to promote sneezing. Persons addicted to snuff were sometimes inaccurately advised to take substances such as pepper as a ptarmic, to make themselves succumb to paroxysms of sneezing, all in the mistaken belief that this might cure them of their snuffy tobacco habit. It did not. What it accomplished was to insure that many jabots and cravats went to the laundry mucus-slimed and snot-flecked.

In many dictionaries the word *ptarmic* immediately preceded the word *ptarmigan*. *Ptarmos* is the Classical Greek noun meaning a sneeze. The echoic Greek verb *ptairein* 'to sneeze' imitates the sound made by a human sneeze. Thus, riffling through the dictionary one sodden eve, after too many flagons of sweet malmsey, some linguistic worthy unacquainted with Gaelic thought the grouse was a sneezing bird and thus—my goodness!—we can't spell it t-a-r-m-i-g-a-n, like those uneducated Scots do. It should have a *p* and be ptarmigan! Egad, sir, riffling does pay off! Actual knowledge of diverse languages be damned! We can guess our way through the dictionary!

I propose then that some keen logophile discovered,

perhaps early in the Age of Enlightenment, the word *ptarmic* soon after he or she had been pondering the origin of the word *tarmigan* and its newer spelling *ptarmigan*. In trying to decide which spelling was correct and what the word's ultimate etymon might be, the logophile was misled by the Greek word and by his own lack of a Scottish Gaelic vocabulary.

Ptosis is a medical word for droopiness of a structure. Prolapse is one of the medical words for droopiness. If your upper eyelid sags down (prolapses) and covers too much of your eye, you have blepharoptosis, possibly due to paralysis of little muscles that lift and close the eyelid. In rarer cases, ptosis may be congenital, caused by missing or malformed ocular structures. The adjective is ptotic. Thus your droppy eyelid is ptotic.

A plastic surgeon can fix you up, so to speak, by performing a reductive blepharoplasty. But remember the plastic proverb that makes such surgeons smile: "Every plasty is a replasty." What they mean is: no matter how exquisitely sutured the tissue, gravity wins. Our poor old human *corpus infirmum* sinks eventually towards *terra firma*.

So the British could not bring themselves to utter the *p* in words like psychology and pseudopod. It is perfectly easy. Children do it for fun the first time they encounter the words. The British, of course, imagined they might sound silly dashing about uttering explosive *p* noises. Little did they know the plosive pleasure of pronouncing the *p* in pterodactyl!

Now let's return to our member of the grouse family. There are three species of ptarmigan in Canada and Alaska: rock, willow, and white-tailed. Some of these grouse make a low, throaty, croaking sound. And that's how Scottish Gaelic speakers named the bird. *Tarmachan* is pronounced TAR-mah-khan. The *ch* in Gaelic is as harsh as a deep-throated cough, as when one hears a true Scot say the word *loch*. Tarmachan means 'croaker' or 'murmurer' in Gaelic. Explorers in our Canadian Arctic report that some ptarmigan croak louder than bullfrogs! *Tarm* is also Gaelic for 'murmur.' More modest ptarmigans murmur as they waddle happily through snowy uplands. And so do some of us tippy canoeists.

Here the canoe tips, as we unload a Canadian word so phoney and spurious that it constitutes a comic scene all by itself. That word is pibloqtok.

Pibloktoq is a dark-of-winter craziness among Inuit people, whose chief symptom is an acute attack of screaming, crying, and running madly through the snow, the episodes of hysterical excitement or frenzy followed by depression or stupor, affecting especially women. Pibloktoq is an Inupiak word, Inupiak being an Inuit-Aleut language spoken in parts of Canada, Alaska, and Greenland.

The older spelling was piblokto. Pibloktoq, the intact Inupiak spelling, is now preferred in psychiatric texts.

As a disorder with a cogent etiology, pibloktoq may not exist. There is some suggestion that white explorers may have "invented" or "imposed" the syndrome. Read on.

Pibloktoq is now a technical term among shrinks, carved in volumes of granitic psychiatric data as authoritative as the *DSM-IV*. This is the *Diagnostic and Statistical Manual of Mental Disorders, Fourth Edition*, published under the not always benign auspices of the American Psychiatric Association.

The *DSM-IV* claims essentially that pibloktoq or arctic hysteria is "an abrupt, dissociative episode accompanied by extreme excitement of up to thirty minutes' duration, frequently followed by convulsive seizures and coma lasting up to twelve hours. The individual may be withdrawn or mildly irritable for a period of hours or days before the attack and will typically report complete amnesia after the attack. During the attack, the individual may tear off his or her clothing, break furniture, shout obscenities, eat feces, flee from protective shelters and run nude across ice and snow, or perform other irrational or dangerous acts."

Humbly your servile author, Wee Willy Casselman, suggests that one such dangerous act may be curling up by the old oil lamp on a winter's eve and spending too many hours reading the *DSM*.

The reader ought to know that a common and valid criticism of the *DSM* is that it seeks to pathologize every single nanosecond of modern life. Are you depressed because you received an "F" in geometry? Look out! It might, soothes the *DSM*, be a depressive disease.

Balderdash! Piffle! Twaddle!

Or common sense may tell one that one merely feels guilty and wants to do better the next time. The next time you are at the library in need of a few laughs, grab the *DSM* and leaf through it briefly. You will be amazed how deeply persistently loony we all are—according to American shrinks.

Lurking in the back pages of the *DSM-IV* is a list of what the authors call "culture-bound syndromes." I call it: oinky white guys pasting nutter labels on non-white persons.

Pibloktoq appears on that list, and so must be treated with extreme skepticism.

In all of psychiatric literature there appear to be a scant 25 case histories of pibloktoq, studied with any reasonable clinical methodology. This citational paucity in the psychiatric literature led one investigator to suggest that the Danish and Norwegian explorers who first reported this "syndrome," including that old bandit explorer Peter Freuchen, misunderstood Inuit women running away screaming from white Arctic travellers themselves. Imagine sex-starved Danish explorer-thugs galumphing and charging toward the aboriginal women.

Ever take a gander at a photograph of Peter Freuchen? Walruses would flee in terror from such an abomination. "He who walks by night" is not too strong an epithet for that mercifully defunct scribe. Freuchen may have coined the other word used in the literature to describe piblok-toq, namely kayaksvimmel. Kayaksvimmel = *kayak* (Inuit canoe) + *svimmel* (Danish, Norwegian) distress, anxiety, dizziness, craziness.

Lyle Dick, the historian, collected all the published accounts of pibloktoq and was the first to suggest that psychiatric case description; he transformed a situation of sexual exploitation of Inuit women by explorers into a discrete disorder worthy of a new diagnostic label. Good for you, Lyle!

Of course, there are culture-bound syndromes, disorders specific to particular locales. As well, culture, belief, and experience do interact in the formation of psychiatric problems. Outer Mongolians in the midst of a famine might be puzzled to see an Alabama cheerleader eating a protein-rich meal and then vomiting it up on purpose. North Americans would shrug and label it bulimia.

One cogent suggestion about the cause of pibloktoq, which may be nothing more or less serious than our "cabin fever," came from a scientist who said it was caused by overdosing on vitamin A. Here's a quote from an abstract of that study:

> Experimental and clinical studies of nonhumans and humans reveal somatic and behavioral effects of hypervitaminosis A which closely parallel many of the symptoms reported for Western patients diagnosed as hysterical and Inuit sufferers of pibloktoq. Eskimo nutrition provides abundant sources of vitamin A and lays the probable basis in some individuals for hyper-vitaminosis A through ingestion of livers, kidneys, and fat of arctic fish and mammals, where the vitamin often is stored in poisonous quantities. Possible con-nections between pibloktoq and hypervitaminosis A are explored. A multifactorial framework may yield a more compelling model of some cases of pibloktoq than those that are mainly unicausal, since, among other things, the disturbance has been reported for males and females, adults and children, and dogs.

Pibloktoq is then a neat word from our Canadian North. But suspicious is the origin of the putative syndrome in psychiatric literature.

My personal canoe of Canuck patience tips when I encounter Canadian words used to deceive the reader. Sneaky, creeping little rat words that try to enter the house of verbal legitimacy by furtive nibbling on its foundations, by choosing word trickery over word clarity. One of the great, feculent swamps from which such slug words of gobbledygook crawl is—naturally—government bureaucracy. That is indeed the stillbirthplace of my all-time, least-favourite Canadian word, nordicity.

The comic scene in this part of Canadian life occurs when such non-words receive official blessing and are accepted without quibble, without as much as a gobble of protest. *Nordicity*, for example, is a headword entry in the *Canadian Oxford Dictionary.* Nordicity, *Oxford* claims, is "a measure of the degree of northernness of a high-latitude place." I'd like to show you that there is much more going on in this deceptive term than *Oxford* ever knew, for in its definition there is not one jot or tittle of demurring negativity suggesting that this is a well-known weasel word laughed about by people who actually know something about Canada's North.

But first, what is gobbledygook?

Gobbledygook is language expressed to deceive, not to inform. Gobbledygook is language wrapped in twaddling clothes and dying in a manger. It is twaddle because it often does not make sense. It's in a manger of the same straw that packs the heads and hearts of those who use it. And it is dying because it is language drained of vital reference. By obscuring common referents to which the listener or reader can attach everyday meaning, bafflegab hopes to slither off into the underbrush of unmeaning before one realizes that nothing has been said. Canadian bureaucrats use it when they need to hide government inaction or mistakes, or when they need to send a canoe full of cow flop up the well-known stream.

No surprise is it to learn that gobbledygook sprang to the lips of a man who had to listen to politicians blabbing. During World War II, Congressman Maury Maverick of Texas made the word up one day in Washington, D.C., after listening to more verbal bamboozlement than he could abide. In May of 1944 Maverick told the *New York Times Magazine*: "Perhaps I was thinking of the old bearded turkey gobbler back in Texas who was always gobbledygobbling and strutting with ludicrous pomposity. At the end of this gobble there was a sort of gook." The new word was so echoic and fitting that it passed immediately into popular speech.

Nordicity

Here's what happened when I encountered the word *nordicity* for the first time. It was unlisted in any dictionary I possessed. A pestering of learned friends drew blank stares. "Not in my vocabulary, old boy," sniffed a pear-shaped polymath from his table at a trendy Toronto eatery, the Donner Party Deli (Today's Special: Mom's Leg of Dad). Now, I pride myself on being as pompous as the next man. Well, all right, the next man happens to be Louis XIV. Folks, I tried humbleness, but I couldn't drop my *h*'s like Uriah Heep. Although I know a number of obscure Canadian words, nordicity flummoxed me—*moi*, fount of all earthly Canadiana, hard drive of compacted verbal wisdom, magneto-optical storage device of gigabytic capaciousness. A brisk riffle through tomes of etymological lore did bring to light the unrelated word *nordicism*, with its spooky image of some blond, blue-eyed psychopath worshipping spruce trees and naming his children Wotan and Yggdrasil and Thor. I see him accompanied by a dirndled milkmaid who pauses under the sprucey boughs to whisper, "Oh Gunnar, I would rather do it with a walrus than put on that helmet again, just so you can get it up."

Do you sense that, in my quest for nordicity, scholarly resolve was melting away? No, I pressed on. I consulted by email the great lexicographer Fred de Gaspy Azmatov, who has not stopped talking since 1961. Okay, once he stopped: May 17, 1973, when a house wren built its nest in his mouth. A last-minute wrenectomy saved him. Fred could offer no definition.

Caution: Dendrasts Ahead!

So I put an ad in a newspaper, only to receive one lone reply from a Fritz Pfropf who wanted me to meet him at the bus station in North Bay, Ontario, whence we would travel deep into the woods to join a coven of dendrasts. Although not found in any dictionary, dendrast is a word derived from two Greek roots, *dendron* 'tree' and *erastes* 'lover.' Dendrasts are persons whose sexual predilections are chiefly arboreal. Fritz put it bluntly: "They whine for the pine; they screech for the beech; they mount the olive." No, dendrasty was not for me. Dendrasts have taken tree-hugging one step beyond, one thrust beyond. I declined the invitation with a postcard: "Sorry, Fritz. Bark would tend to abrade the penile epidermis. And, as a gentleman, I do not propose to play hide-the-sausage with a knothole."

Then, at last, reality! Lexical pay dirt! In *The Canadian Encyclopedia* under the headword *nordicity* was a coloured map and a very long entry by Louis-Edmond Hamelin, author of *Nordicité canadienne* (1975, revised 1980, translated in 1979 as *Canadian Nordicity: It's Your North Too*).

Now I was getting somewhere, namely, smack dab into a cat's cradle of Canadian geographical gobbledygook. Nordicity is an index of northernness that calculates and quantifies certain polar values, criteria shortformed as VAPO. True, I have always longed to quantify, but the closest I ever came was to Qantasfly on that trip to Australia. VAPO is an acronym of French origin, from the initial letters of *valeur polaire*, 'polar value.'

With chagrin I discovered that, according to nordicity quantification, I dwell below the dread isonord (a line on a map joining points that have equal VAPO) that is the limit of "Base Canada." I live where I was born in the pleasant town of Dunnville, Ontario. A few miles hence, the Grand River empties its modest billows into Lake Erie.

My Dunnville home, therefore, has a VAPO index of nil. Zero. Nada. Rien. Nichts. Do I therefore repine? Do I mope? No, I do not sulk. I will bear my town's VAPO index of zero like a man—a bedraggled, broken homunculus, yes—after delving into nordicity, but still, a man.

Nordicity Explained

Please, class, sit up straight. Here comes the heavy-duty McCoy. The polar value (VAPO) criteria (geographical and human) are ten in number: variables like latitude, summer heat, annual cold, types of ice, accessibility by land, air service, resident population, economic activities, and availability of licorice all-sorts by arctic rescue helicopter.

Yeah, yeah, I made the last one up. Sorry.

Now pay attention. Each VAPO criterion is expressed on a scale of 0 to 100. The North Pole has VAPO to the max, dude. Its index is 10 X 100 = 1,000. Churchill, Manitoba, in the Middle North has a VAPO of 450; Yellowknife, 390 VAPO; the centre of Hudson Bay, 622 VAPO; Alert, NWT, 878 VAPO; Red Lake, Ontario, 220 VAPO.

Right. And Jack Frost's dick has a VAPO of 6.

Turning aside from the contemplation of nordicity, we look now at the language in which this "science" is couched. In his engrossing article in *The Canadian Encyclopedia*, Mr. Hamelin writes sentences like these:

- "Nordicity does increase abruptly above isonord 200."
- "A quantitative denordification of approximately 25% has occurred" [in the last century].
- "At least 2 categories of nordicities of exploitation must be identified: nordicity of use and normative nordicity."

- "Many activities in the North seem to have been determined by . . . the inadequate appreciation of Amerindian ethnicity." (Could he mean by screwing the natives?)

Class, do not confuse such writing with clear expression.

By using nordicity criteria, writes the author, "nordic space occupies about 70% of Canada's territory. This seems a more exact estimate than the official 39%." Here we reach a crux of the presentation and perhaps the true reason for the creation of nordicity. By using the nordicity system, geographers interested in the North can claim they are devoting their attentions to much more than half of Canada. This comes in mighty handy at government-handout time, when geographers go begging for federal grants. Even in the dankest pits of obfuscatory gibberish, always look for the buck.

Nordicity can be quite fairly viewed as a cool tool to assist in the economic exploitation of the North. Mr. Hamelin himself points out that it has already been used to make up a wage scale for certain workers in our North (sorry, in our norddom), in predicting tourist traffic (of a nordoid direction), and in a study by the Fisheries Board of Canada. His Nordship then adds: "This index would provide a more realistic basis for determining royalty zones in the development of northern petroleum than does the simple division by latitude now used." I think Northern residents can detect the possible devastation in that remark. Or am I a nord? Sorry, a nerd?

Uses of Jargon
The making of new words is a sign that a language is vital.

But never be under the illusion that because a new label has been plastered on something, because it has been dubbed with a scrap of pseudo-scientific jargon, we somehow will know it more deeply.

On the other hand, all sciences need a private vocabulary. Some jargon is necessary. In one sense, all professional terminology is jargon, including that of medicine, law, education, business, sports, theology, etc., because the unique word-hoards of these fields contain terms not familiar to the general population. Linguists estimate that one-half of the vocabulary of all major world languages consists of scientific and technical terms. In Modern English, with more items of vocabulary than any other language that has existed, technical vocabulary makes up closer to 80 percent of all words.

More Nordicity

These private technical vocabularies often contain words composed of roots from classical Latin and Greek. Nordicity appears to have been coined in French first, so it has a suffix that forms many abstract nouns in French, namely *-icité*. *Nordicité* apes French nouns like *publicité*. English borrowed *publicité* as publicity, and it acquired a new meaning. *Publicité* was formed as if from a Latin noun *publicitas* 'public-ness.' As it happens, the abstract noun stems from the French adjective *publique*, but the noun was formed to imitate noun-making precedents derived from Latin. This particular suffix was much used in Latin to form feminine abstract nouns ending in *-tas, -tatis*. Examples still in English include vanity fron *uanitas* and liberty from *libertas*.

Why Use Latin & Greek?

As one expects, science requires a large number of new nouns naming various abstractions, objects, and processes. To tag these verbal concepts, science goes back to classical Latin and Greek when making the new words it needs. And that suggests a question: Why use those 'dead' languages to form scientific and technical terms? First, there is historical precedent. We have borrowed such words into English since the birth of the language. Second, in a dead language the meaning of a word does not change. It is semantically frozen. It is crystallized in obsolescence. But in a living language, words acquire new meanings. In 1930, *acid* meant a chemical like the acetic acid in vinegar. By the middle of the 1960s, acid had added yet another meaning: it could refer in English slang to LSD, a dangerous hallucinogenic drug. That new meaning spawned other new terms like *acidhead* and *bad acid trip*. Like healthy tissue, language is organic: it grows; it sheds old word cells and creates new ones.

Because precise meaning and precise use of words is crucial in all forms of scientific communication, it helps to be able to make new words from Latin and Greek roots which themselves always mean the same thing. The Greek root *acro-* will always mean 'high' and *phobos* will always mean 'fear,' so acrophobia will always mean 'morbid fear of heights.' Makers of new scientific words don't have to worry about *acro-* acquiring a new meaning. Classical Greek is a dead language. The root meanings cannot change, as they can in English. We ought to note here that Modern Greek is a vibrant tongue, still very much alive in Greece and wherever in the world Greek people gather.

By the way, knowing *acro-* helps in ordinary English word origins too. An acrobat was first a high-wire walker, a walker on ropes strung across a room or a street. The high, defended part of an ancient Greek city was an acropolis from Greek *polis* 'city.' Athens had the most famous one. Can you guess what and where the Acrocorinth was?

One final reason we use Latin and Greek roots to form scientific words is—believe it or not—they make terms that are shorter and more convenient than long descriptions in English. Let's take one example from medicine. Yes, medical words are daunting, even frightening, if you've never encountered them. Big, polysyllabic jawbreakers like cholecystostomy are not part of everyday English. However, cholecystostomy is much quicker and easier to write than its definition in English: namely, the surgical making of a mouth-like opening (Greek *stoma*) in the wall of the gall (Greek *chole*) bladder (Greek *cysto-*) to introduce a catheter for the purpose of draining excess fluid accumulation. Greek and Latin terms provide a kind of shorthand for the description of complex objects and procedures in medicine and many other sciences. Personally, I'll take cholecystostomy any day. Now that I know the simple Greek roots, I can even remember more easily how to spell the word.

Nordicity, My Felicity!

In the last analysis, nordicity is similar to other new concepts. It too will have its fate in the verbal marketplace. Nordicity has already been lollygagging in the foyers of geographic academe since the 1960s. It may be here to stay.

New terms are minted and then must brave circulation. Some will endure, some fracture, some fall into disuse and oblivion.

But long, technical words do not always spring from practical or noble motives. Sometimes they pepper academic writing because the author is insecure and needs to impress the reader. Sometimes the very science is new. When educational sociology was in verbal diapers, it spewed forth silly, polysyllabic jargon at a dictionary-boggling rate—still does, from time to time.

In the end, of course, one does want to be fair-minded. By all means, give nordicity every chance. Even I am trying to adopt the right norditude. Let's see now. I'll conserve strength by not taking part in communal northern sex (a nordgy). I'll try to express this in language worthy of those who write about nordicity. By extrapolation, from the conjecturally applicable variables is manifest the incontrovertible substantiation of one further, pertinent—um—guess: perhaps nordicity does herald an advance in techniques of biogeographical measurement? With thumping heart I await fresh vistas of insight with the advent of concepts like westment, eastacy, and southiza-tionment.

And, while waiting here in my fur booties and parka, I certainly plan at all costs to avoid hypernordosis of the buttocks.

As for the scourge of multinorditiveness in the common geographical article, well, that's a whole other kettle of—ichthyonordic entities.

*The following is a comic scene from Canadian life for me,
indeed, for all of us who are scared silly at the prospect of
climbing giant iced rockfaces to obtain glory. Les* québécois
coined a new name word about eight years ago, Festiglace
du Québec.

Festiglace as a compound word is a blend of *le festival* 'festival' and *la glace* 'ice.' The French word stems from Latin
glacies 'ice.' *Le festival* and *le festin* 'feast, banquet' are
French words derived ultimately from the Latin adjective
festus 'solemn, festal, pertaining to a religious ceremony.'
How very fitting that a derivative of a religious adjective
like *festus* should adorn now in our secular age a ceremony where ice walls are climbed while persons gather
below to scream. On second thought, it's not so far from
some religious ceremonies as we might at first believe.

    La Festiglace du Québec was the world's largest ice-
climbing event, held from February 18 to 20, 2005, on the
spectacular walls of the Jacques-Cartier River in Pont-
Rouge located some 20 minutes by car from Quebec City.

    The ice cascades of the Jacques-Cartier River canyon
played host to this international competition where
famous climbers and outdoor enthusiasts met to cele-
brate their passion for ice-climbing. Courses, kiosks,
training sessions, introductions to ice climbing, snow-
shoeing circuits, equipment demos, Tyrolean traverses, a

kids' zone, evening lectures, international and amateur competitions—all were part of *Festiglace.*

Les québécois coined new words to describe winter below and above the St. Lawrence River, and they also extended the meanings of European French words. Thus, *la bordée* acquires the new Canadian sense of 'a heavy snowfall,' whereas in 16th-century France the word began lexical life as a term for a line of cannons ranged along one side of a ship. *La bordée* also meant firing these cannons in unison to deliver a broadside.

Ice piled up on riverbanks or shores of lakes is *bordage* or *bordillon.* Quebeckers created *banc de neige* 'snow bank,' and *bouette* 'melting snow.' Wintry verbs have burgeoned forth too. *Botter* means to get one's shoes or boots all gummed up with packed snow. *Embourber* is to get a car stuck in the snow. The reflexive verb *s'embourber* is to sink into the snow oneself.

Neige 'snow' gives the *québécoise* neology *neigeailler* in which the root takes the common diminutive verbal ending '*-ailler*' to produce the useful impersonal form *il neigeaille* 'it's snowing a little' or 'it's just a light dusting of snow.'

If you have to make a road across a frozen lake or river, you might set broken-off branches of pine or spruce into the ice to indicate where the course of the road will be even after a winter storm covers the roadway itself. Such a marker line is called une *balise* in Quebec. In France it's a word for buoy, and in France *baliser* means to mark out a water channel with beacons or to equip an airport runway with approach lights. These meanings of *baliser* are used in Quebec as well.

Frazil

A Quebec word borrowed into Canadian Maritime English is frasil or *frazil*, for the slushy-chunky floes of small ice pieces that move on the surface of running water early in the spring. It might begin as a French word for cinders, *frasil*. It might stem from the verb *fraiser*, to shell beans. It appears in English as frazil or frazzle ice. Quebec French could have borrowed it from frazzle, which can mean 'to fray, to come undone.'

Here's an extra note, from the University of Guelph: **FRAZIL**: "The first stage in river ice formation is when crystals start to form and grow. But the water movement interrupts crystal growth and the crystals don't join together to form a sheet. Instead you get a mixture of ice crystals and water that looks like a wet slushie. The crystals are called frazil and the mixture of crystals and water is called frazil slush."

For Fans of Latin Etymology Only

Webster's Third New International Dictionary, Unabridged (Merriam-Webster, 2002) offers an intriguing guess at the derivation of *frasil* as the French word for 'cinders.'

They posit an origin of French *fraisil* 'coal cinders' as an alteration of Old French faisil; it comes from an assumed form in Vulgar Latin like **facilis*, from Latin *fax fac-*, Latin 'torch' + *-ilis* '–ile,' a common Latin adjectival suffix of pertinence. Note that this **facilis* would be—if it ever existed—a homonym of the common Latin adjective *facilis* 'easy' that gives us the English and French *facile* 'easy to do.'

By the way, if you are new to etymology, the asterisk *

(*asteriskos* Greek 'little star') before a word indicates a form that has no printed proof, a word form that is hypothetical—someone THINKS it may have existed.

The problems with this supposition are two and they are major. There is not a jot or tittle of printed evidence of this putative *facilis*. The infixing of an *r* in words similar to *facilis* to produce sought-after intermediate forms like *fracilis* and *fracile* and *frasile* is otherwise unknown in French etymology. The questing word-sleuth ought to view with great suspicion all such derivational singularities. They do happen. Language is alive as it evolves. But exceptions to the broad rules are passing rare. The things the Gallic tongue did to street Latin tend to be similar.

Derivation follows rules based on studying both the original Latin word and then observing what happened to the Latin word as it was borrowed and changed into an Early French word. The morphology of Late Latin as it is transformed into Old French has been well studied and one might almost say quantified. Transformational rules applicable to the Romance languages are available in many linguistics textbooks and are worth study by any obsessed word nut.

What is Vulgar Latin?
Vulgar Latin does not mean, as one cheerful email to me suggested, "that those ancient Romans were very foul-mouthed." Vulgar Latin was a variety of the Proto-Romance language, spoken in Northern Italy, Gaul, the Iberian Peninsula, and Northern Africa, whose speakers by the time of the fall of the Roman Empire in the West numbered approximately 20 million.

As the Roman Empire fell apart and the Christian Church rose to be the hard, social glue holding southern and western Europe together, communication and education declined and regional variation in pronunciation and grammar increased until gradually after about 600 CE, local forms of Western Romance (Vulgar Latin) were no longer mutually intelligible. After about 650 CE, the various dialects of Vulgar Latin are considered separate Romance languages.

The *Third Merriam-Webster Dictionary* defines it thus: "Vulgar Latin was the nonclassical Latin of ancient Rome including both the speech of plebeians and the informal daily speech of educated Romans that is scantily recorded in literature but attested by inscriptions and established by comparative evidence as the chief source of the Romance languages."

A RISLEY ACT
A Real Term in Showbiz Slang

A Risley act gave me the biggest, deepest, best-remembered laugh of my life. I was in the audience and on the stage was a Risley act. My friend Jim Guthro, musician, composer, and long-time executive in the Canadian Broadcasting Corporation's TV Variety Department introduced me to this phrase.

Jim Guthro writes, "I first heard the term *a Risley act* from a Toronto agent and booker named Joey Poster. Joey could talk only if he took the labially disfigured cigar out of his mouth. He was a character; about 5 feet tall and 5 feet wide. As agent he booked acts at the Barclay Hotel, a half-star joint in Toronto, as well as the Prince Arthur, the Casino, and during its final years, the Victory Burlesque Theatre on Spadina. Some of the quasi-vaudeville acts Joey Poster booked would turn up on TV in the early and mid-fifties, including on *The Ed Sullivan Show*."

Webster's Dictionary says the American term from 19th-century showbiz was named "after the Risley family, a 19th-century circus trio consisting of Richard Risley Carlisle, died 1874, American gymnast and circus performer, and his two sons" and that it is "a circus act in which an acrobat lying on his back juggles barrels or fellow acrobats with his feet."

However, by the 1920s, in the colourful argot of vaudeville and booking-agent slang a comic twist was added. In the vaudeville extension of its meaning, "a Risley" referred to a showbiz act that deliberately went bad. The performance began as a legitimate acrobatic presentation, and then suddenly, a minute or two into it, the acrobat lying on the floor fumbled the one being juggled and he or she dropped down and crushed the guy on the floor.

Depending on the imagination of the performers, a Risley act can proceed to worsen to utter chaos. There you see the beginnings of certain vaudeville comedy turns such as the Ritz Brothers, the Marx Brothers, and Olsen & Johnson in 'Hellzapoppin.' By extension then, the term began to be applied by the late twenties and well into the fifties to a failed act that went wrong for deliberate comic effect. That's how I first encountered a Risley act and saw the funniest performance I have ever seen.

His stage name was Carl Ballantine, sometimes billed as the "Great Ballantine." On CBS's long-running 1950s variety program *The Ed Sullivan Show,* Carl was the "Amazing Mr. Ballantine." He was the first performer who reduced me to a laughing jag so powerful that I rolled on the rug of our living room, my sides aching from persistent laughter and my jaw muscles stretched to the snapping point, all from watching Ballantine on *Ed Sullivan.*

Just a few months later, I saw Carl Ballantine live on the Borscht Belt Circuit. While visiting my wonderful Aunt Eleanore in New York City, I was invited by Jewish friends to a resort in the Catskill Mountains. The Borscht Belt was a collective phrase for large summer resorts in the Catskills visited by Jewish New Yorkers in the 1950s and 1960s. Movies such as *Dirty Dancing* and *A Walk on the Moon* depict these big hotels, where comedians such as Sid Caesar, Jerry Lewis, Lenny Bruce, Buddy Hackett, and Jackie Mason worked early in their careers. These summer hotels included Brown's, the Concord, Grossinger's, Kutscher's, the Nevele, the Pines, the Raleigh, and the Windsor.

On my first weekend at a Catskill resort, the Friday night headliner was Fat Jack Leonard, the world's nastiest and funniest insult comedian. Fat Jack's *habañero* invective made Don Rickles' later wimpish chops seem like those of a choirboy. But Saturday night was the prize, the funniest live theatre I have ever seen in my years on earth. It will be difficult to describe Carl Ballantine's act and make it seem in any manner as deeply and originally funny as it was. But I can give a taste of the best Risley act I ever saw.

Carl Ballantine in 1964 was a member of the cast of the popular TV sitcom *McHale's Navy*. Needless to say, on the dorky sitcom Ballantine's comic potential was wasted. But that's how he looked the night I almost died laughing at his magic act. He wore the proper black tie and tails of the stage magician that evening.

Ballantine, born Meyer Kessler, did a magic act. But none of his tricks worked. The Amazing Mr. Ballantine's every magic trick would begin well and then flop. A deftly fanned pack of cards would suddenly stick together and explode in a loud *splat!* all over the stage floor. The diaphanous thrill of a silken scarf seemingly plucked from infinity would suddenly stick in the false thumb tip where it had been rolled. Smiling weakly, Carl would give the reluctant-to-emerge scarf a delicate tug with one hand and with the other arm execute the confident magician's wave of abracadabra! The scarf stayed stuck. Nothing. With an even weaker smile the magician would yank the scarf so hard that his false thumb tip would come off, fall to the stage floor, and roll noisily into the orchestra pit with a pert *ping!* Carl would stare sadly as the pathetic fake plastic thumb tip sank into the orchestra pit. Then, smiling the brave trooper smile that every failing vaudeville performer has smiled throughout the history of showbiz, Carl would plunge enthusiastically into his next marvel of prestidigitation.

"Voilà! The golden ball! Under which of these three alabaster cups will this gilded sphere reside when at last I have completed my shuffling of the cups?" Trumpet flourish. Each cup is lifted. The golden spheroid has decamped. It is not under any of the cups. Where is it? Carl opens his hands, pulls out the pockets of his now gently shredding black tie and tails. Beads of sweat wreathe the magician's brow. He wipes them away with one of the silken scarves. The blue colour in the cheap scarf comes off on Carl's forehead. With the old two-chord revelation ta-DAAAAAH! Carl shows his sleeves. No golden ball. He takes off his corsage and shakes it. Zilch. Gingerly he pulls up his trouser legs, shows his socks, turns out the cuffs of his pants. The music stops. Carl now permits himself a frown. He walks across the stage to get a small table for the next magic trick. The golden ball drops out of his pants with a loud click and rolls slowly, slowly, slowly toward the orchestra pit. Carl bows his head in prayer. The audience screams with laughter. So do I.

Only mildly flustered, Carl Ballantine walks hesitantly to the side of the stage where a large cardboard placard states in large letters: "Tonight! Amazing Carl Ballantine! Sleight of Hand Magic!" With a long face, Carl takes out a thick felt marker and changes a word. Now the sign reads: "Slight of Hand."

Never mind. The show must go on. Ballantine, to a trumpet flourish, a drum roll, and a rim shot from the pit band, draws forth the rabbit from the top hat.

The rabbit is dead.

Ballantine would then begin a comic dialogue in which he berated the dead rabbit. On the night in the Catskills when I nearly expired in mid-guffaw, Ballantine veered off into a 20-minute existential rant of epic proportions. First, the dead "prop" rabbit was wonderfully floppy and bunnylike and truly sad-looking. Second, Ballantine became slowly angry with the dead rabbit but in a resigned, mournful manner that added to the comic poignancy. "I trained you. I fed you carrots (a strangled sob). I got you an introduction to Thumper. Ingrate! *Goyishe* rabbit! Gourmet carrots yet! Not little orange shitty sticks from poverty. We're talkin': A CARROT. And how do you thank me? By dying? Bastard! I bet you're workin' on your own act, after I leave the theatre at night, is that it? Yeah! You're going on *The Steve Allen Show* next week as 'The Hare That Wasn't There.' Putz!" Here the Amazing Mr. Ballantine began to lightly cuff the dead rabbit and slap its impudent face. "You think it's all over, Bugs? Is that it? The weeping, the gnashing of incisors. The sitting Shiva for my wallet? I have ways to punish you. Ever heard of a hare shirt, buddy? Huh?"

The shtick then sailed further out of the bounds of daily sense, out, out, into a dizzy stratosphere of exquisite Ballantine nonsense. But underneath it all was the sober, stark fact that life was like this. Sometimes the rabbit is dead. Sometimes the new house burns to the ground. The shiny new Buick, left in neutral, careens over the cliff. The hot-to-trot babe you picked up tonight at The Club Foot is a man named Abner Stenson who sells mufflers during the week in Erie, Pennsylvania. After all the lessons, yes, even for Canadians, the canoe does tip.

Wherever you are, Carl Ballantine, thank you for the biggest, deepest, best-remembered laugh of my life.

MORE BILL CASSELMAN BOOKS
ABOUT CANADIAN WORDS
FROM McARTHUR & COMPANY

CASSELMAN'S CANADIAN WORDS

In this #1 Best-Seller, Bill Casselman delights and startles with word stories from every province and territory of Canada. Did you know that *Scarborough* means "Harelip's Fort"? The names of *Lake Huron & Huronia* stem from a vicious, racist insult. Huron in old French meant 'long-haired clod.' French soldiers labelled the Wendat people with this nasty misnomer in the 1600s. *To deke out* is a Canadian verb that began as hockey slang, short for 'to decoy an opponent.' Canada has a fish that ignites. On our Pacific coast, the oolichan or *candlefish* is so full of oil it can be lighted at one end and used as a candle. "*Mush! Mush!* On, you huskies!" cried Sergeant Preston of The Yukon to 1940s radio listeners, thus introducing a whole generation of Canucks to the word once widely used in the Arctic to spur on sled dogs. Although it might sound like a word from Inuktitut, early French trappers first used it, borrowing the term from the Canadian French command to a horse to go: *Marche! Marche!* Yes, it's Québécois for giddyap!

All these and more fascinating terms from Canadian place names, politics, sports, plants and animals, clothing. Everything from Canadian monsters to mottoes is here.

Casselman's Canadian Words
ISBN 0-7730-5515-0
224 pages, illustrated

Should you purchase a copy of *Casselmania*? Below, dear reader, is a quiz to try. If you pass, buy *Casselmania*. If you fail, buy two copies!

1. "Slackers" is a nickname for what Canadian city?

(a) Vancouver

(b) Halifax

(c) Sackville, New Brunswick

Answer: (b) Why "Slackers"? Because often when Canadian Navy crews put in to Halifax harbour, the sailors had some "slack" time for shore leave.

2. *Eh?* is a true marker of Canadian speech. But which of the following authors uses eh? exactly as Canadians now use it?

(a) Emily Brontë in *Wuthering Heights*

(b) Charles Dickens in *Bleak House*

(c) Geoffrey Chaucer in *The Canterbury Tales* in AD 1400

Answer: All of the above! *Eh?* is almost 1,000 years old as an interjection in Old English, Middle English, and, of course, in modern Canadian English too.

3. The first *Skid Row* or *Skid Road* in Canada was in Vancouver at the end of the 19th century. The term originated because:

(a) Alcoholics kept slipping in the muddy streets

(b) Out-of-work loggers drank in cheap saloons at the end of a road used to skid logs

(c) Cheap houses were moved on skids to slummy areas

Answer: (b). Skids were greased logs used to slide rough timber to a waterway or railhead. There was a skid road in Vancouver, where unemployed loggers waited for jobs, and took the odd bottle of liquid refreshment.

Casselmania: More Wacky Canadian Words & Sayings

ISBN 0-316-13314-0

298 pages, illustrated

CANADIAN GARDEN WORDS

Trowel in hand, Bill Casselman digs into the loamy lore and fascinating facts about how we have named the plants that share our Dominion. But are there *Canadian Garden Words*? Yes! Try those listed below.

Camas Lily is a bulb grown all over the world for its spiky blue flowers. The name arose in British Columbia where First Peoples cooked and ate the bulbs. Camas means 'sweet' in Nootka, a Pacific Coast language. The original name of Victoria on Vancouver Island was Camosun, in Nootka 'place where we gather camas bulbs.'

A *Snotty Var* is a certain species of fir tree in Newfoundland. Why? Find out in *Canadian Garden Words*.

Mistletoe! So Christmassy. The word means 'poop on a stick.' Oops! Look within for a bounty of surprising origins of plant names. Orchid means 'testicle' in Greek. So does avocado. While plant names have come into English from dozens of world languages, Bill Casselman has found the Canadian connection to 100s of plant names and garden lore and packed this book with them. Casselman reports on Canadian plant names and on the origin of all the common trees and flowers that decorate our gardens from Fogo Island to Tofino, B.C.

Canadian Garden Words
ISBN 0-316-13343-4
356 pages, illustrated

CANADIAN FOOD WORDS

Winner Gold Medal Culinary Book of the Year Award for 1999 from Cuisine Canada

"A glorious, informative, and funny collection of
food-related definitions and stories!"
—Marion Kane, food editor, *Toronto Star*

"Even readers who are unlikely to fry a doughnut in seal
blubber oil will enjoy this latest romp by writer and
broadcaster Bill Casselman . . . he mixes in so much
entertaining information and curious Canadian lore."
—Books, *Globe & Mail*

Do you know that fine Canadian dish, *Son-of-a-Bitch-in-a-Sack*? It's a real Alberta chuck wagon pudding. In this fully
illustrated, 304-page romp, Bill tells the amusing stories behind
such hearty Canadian fare as *gooeyducks* and *hurt pie*. The juicy
lore and tangy tales of foods that founded a nation are all here:
from *scrunchins* to *rubbaboo*, from *bangbelly* to *poutine*, from
Winnipeg jambusters to *Nanaimo bars*, from *Malpeque oysters*
to *nun's farts!* If you think foods of Canadian origin are limited to pemmican and pea soup, you need to dip your ladle into
the bubbling kettle of *Canadian Food Words*.

Canadian Food Words
The Juicy Lore and Tasty Origins of Foods that Founded a Nation
ISBN 1-55278-018-X
304 pages, illustrated

Canadian Sayings

**62 weeks on *The National Post*
Top Ten Canadian Non-Fiction List!**

Samples of Canadian sayings from Bill's best-selling book:

- She's got more tongue than a Mountie's boot.
- That smell would gag a maggot on a gut wagon.
- I've seen more brains in a Manitoba sucked egg.
- He's thicker than a B.C. pine stump.
- Saskatchewan is so flat, you can watch your dog run away from home for a week.
- He's so dumb he thinks Medicine Hat is a cure for head lice.
- Sign in bathroom where husband shaves: Warning— Objects in mirror are dumber than they appear.
- Of childish behaviour in a grown man: That boy never did grow up. One day, he just sorta haired over.

There is a reason this book made Canadians chuckle for more than a best-selling year. Buy it and find out why, as you laugh along with what one reviewer called "the funniest Canadian book I've ever read!"

Canadian Sayings
1,200 Folk Sayings Used by Canadians, Collected & Annotated by Bill Casselman
ISBN 1-55278-076-7
138 pages

What's in a Canadian Name?
The Origins & Meanings of Canadian Surnames

From Atwood to Applebaum, from Bobak to Bullard, with Gabereau, Hanomansing, Harnoy, Krall, Tobin, and Shamas tossed into the linguistic salad of our last names, Bill Casselman tells here the fascinating story of surnames, of how humans came to use last names, and of what some last names mean, names that every Canadian knows. Did you know that pop singer Shania Twain bears an Ojibwa first name that means 'on my way'? Movie star Keanu Reeves has a first name that is Hawaiian for 'cool breeze.' Talk show host Mike Bullard's last name is Middle English for 'trickster.' Surnames can trick and surprise you too. Byron sounds sooo uppercrust, doesn't it? Proud family moniker of the famous English poet, etc. Too bad Byron means "at the cowsheds" from Old English byrum and suggests a family origin not in a stately home but in a stately stable! More surprises and delights await any Canadian reader interested in genealogy and surnames.

What's in a Canadian Name?
The Origins & Meanings of Canadian Surnames
ISBN 1-55278-141-0
250 pages

Canadian Sayings 2

"Bill Casselman, bluenose among schooners on the sea of popular etymology, moors his mighty vessel, nets a-teeming with Canadian words." —*Indigo Internet review*

Canadian Sayings 2 was on the National Post Top-Ten Paperback List for 61 weeks!

Canada's funniest collector of salty sayings is back! He's got more than 1,000 new sayings used by Canadians, expressions not in the first volume of *Canadian Sayings*. As usual, Bill has been careful about the limits of good taste. So you'll find old saws like these:

- We were so poor, we never had decorations on the Christmas tree unless Grandpa sneezed.
- Tongue-tied? That dude couldn't adlib a fart at a bean supper.
- The gene pool around here could use a little chlorine.

Yes, Casselman keeps his customary firm grip on decorum and refinement by such offerings as these:

- Toronto woman to her girlfriend at a trendy café: "Sure, I understand about premature ejaculation, but I've been vaccinated slower than that."
- What are you going to do for a face when the monkey wants its ass back?

Would some of these sayings make a corpse blush? The author sincerely hopes not. But only the reader can tell. So check out Volume 2 right now!

Canadian Sayings 2
1,000 Folk Sayings Used by CanadiansNewly Collected and Annotated by Bill Casselman
ISBN 1-55278-272-7
168 pages

"Bill Casselman is one of Canada's foremost lexicographers and word hounds. In addition to a career as a broadcaster and producer for CBC, he is the author of nine books on Canadian language."

—Jennifer MacLennan, *Inside Language: A Canadian Language Reader*

I'm back with fresh bounty: hundreds and hundreds of **new** folk sayings not collected in the previous two volumes. Here's one of my favourites sent in by a Prairie high school class:

- Why is it so windy in Saskatchewan?
  Because Alberta blows and Manitoba sucks.

Hey, it's simple high school geophysics with a touch of chauvinism.

Put-downs are as plentiful as ever:

- If his IQ were any lower, we'd have to water him.
- She'd try to sneak sunrise past a rooster.

There are newly collected Canadian threats too:

- You're lookin' to spit Chiclets, Dude.

This is mock goon talk from a junior hockey arena. Chiclets are little white pieces of chewing gum vaguely toothlike in shape. So the implication is: I'm going to knock your teeth out.

But this collection, like the best-selling previous two books, has praise to offer also:

- That dude could stickhandle through a box of matches.

Canadian Sayings 3
1,000 Folk Sayings Used by Canadians Newly Collected & Annotated by Bill Casselman
ISBN: 1-55278-425-8
174 pages

All Bill Casselman's books are available from online booksellers and at bookstores across Canada.